THE
UNKNOWN ARCHITECTS
OF CIVIL RIGHTS

Thaddeus Stevens, Ulysses S. Grant, and Charles Sumner

Barry M. Goldenberg

CRITICAL MINDS PRESS

Published by Critical Minds Press in Los Angeles, CA

© 2011 by Critical Minds Press

All pictures acquired from the Library of Congress
Cover Design by Barry M. Goldenberg

ISBN-13 978-0615504582
ISBN-10 0615504582

Library of Congress Control Number: 2011916687

Printed in the United States of America

For all the teachers who have inspired me

—and believed in me—

both past and present

ACKNOWLEDGEMENTS

ACKNOWLEDGEMENTS

This book would not exist without Professor Joan Waugh, my honors thesis advisor at UCLA. When I originally approached her about undertaking an honors thesis during my final year as an undergraduate, I had little clue as to what I actually would write about in the mid-nineteenth century time period of American History. While my topic changed many times, Professor Waugh was able to steer me toward a topic that was one of my greatest life passions—civil rights. Nine months later, she helped me craft this original and exciting yet unfocused idea into a full-fledged, coherent thesis that I sincerely believe adds to the rich—and very abundant—historical literature on U.S. Civil Rights History. Yet, the entire writing process would never have been possible without her vast amount of knowledge that she shared with me every step of the way. In addition, the passion she has for this same subject matter was extremely contagious and only motivated me to produce the best thesis possible.

To be able to learn from an extraordinary, accomplished historian and intellectual has been an invaluable academic experience. I am extremely fortunate to have had her guiding me during the writing of this thesis—now my very own book—as I am indebted to her in so many ways. So Professor Waugh, thank you for your extraordinary patience, your dedication to me, your constant guidance, your brilliant insight, and your endless support.

But more importantly, thank you for your continued enthusiasm towards my thesis, your constant warmth, and above all, your remarkable kindness. You are the epitome of what an educator should be—brilliant yet genuine, challenging yet understanding, and always caring for my wellbeing not just in school but also in life. As I begin my own journey into Academia, you are truly a role model who I will always admire. Thank you for everything.

It would be remiss of me to leave out thanking my best friend, Ashley, for being my rock when I wrote this thesis. Thank you for all the endless encouragement and motivation during the long nights I spent writing and researching. I may not have finished without you! And of course, thank you for all your editing, constant suggestions, aiding me with the cover design, helping me in the library, and just investing yourself in making this the best it could be despite your own busy schedule and workload.

Of course, thank you to my family—my grandparents, brother, aunts and uncles, cousins, and lastly, my parents. Your love and support throughout my life and now in my academic pursuits continues to motivate me each and every day. You are my inspiration—I love you all.

As I write this section over a year since I initially started on this journey, I am proud to present these words no longer as a passionate idea that evolved into an undergraduate thesis, but as my first book that, while imperfect, is a powerful, important, and timeless story of three men who stood up—and risked their careers—against the injustices of their time. America's history has always been defined as an on-going progressive process towards "a more perfect" union. Stevens, Grant, and Sumner each played important parts in that process that still continues today. From the bottom of my heart, thank you for reading—these three men deserve it.

Barry Goldenberg
Los Angeles, California
August 1, 2011

Contents

The
Unknown Architects
of Civil Rights

PREFACE

Throughout the history of the United States, the struggle for civil rights, equality, and adherence to the principles of freedom has been—and will forever be—an intricate part of the American narrative. This book examines a specific time in that narrative, Reconstruction (1865-1877), and highlight how the achievements of three men helped produce America's first civil rights movement. While there are many men and women who contributed to the important civil rights gains during the Reconstruction era, Pennsylvania Congressman Thaddeus Stevens, Massachusetts Senator Charles Sumner, and President Ulysses S. Grant were three of the most influential men who were responsible for the first major legislation ensuring black equality.

In addition, not only were these three men influential, but they were also three of the most famous—or infamous—Americans that lived during this time period. For example, historian Joan Waugh explained President Grant's "larger-than-life legacy" in which, "a million and a half people gathered in New York City to view the funeral procession and burial ceremonies."[1] In the case of Thaddeus Stevens, contemporary Alexander Hood wrote a biography shortly after the Congressman's death and declared Stevens as "one of the great American statesmen, towering high above the millions around him."[2]

Charles Sumner, too, was not only hailed as a martyr in the North, but considered "the foremost man in the civil service of the United States."[3]

However, make no mistake; each of these men had both political and personal flaws—some more detrimental than others—and during this time period, Stevens and Sumner were each considered radical by some and Grant was often considered to be an inefficient and corrupt president. None of these men were saints nor should they be remembered as such as they were chosen more for their legislative impacts than their personalities. Yet, given the sharply divided political environment following the Civil War, Thaddeus Stevens, Charles Sumner, and Ulysses S. Grant were indeed staunch advocates for black equality at a time when holding such a view was not only extreme, but downright dangerous and politically suicidal. In addition, each was independent of each other; while interaction existed between the three in various capacities, they were *not* linked together in a cohesive civil rights movement but instead acted separately for what they thought was in the best interest of the country. The two big themes of Reconstruction, reunion and emancipation, played into those interests with Grant focusing on the former and Stevens and Sumner on the latter. However, as they each learned, those two causes were tightly intertwined. Frankly, Stevens and Sumner both displayed incredible foresight toward racial equality and put their careers at risk fighting on blacks' behalf. While racial equality was not necessarily the goal of President Grant's administration, Grant's main goal was to reunite the country, and he felt that granting full rights to African Americans was vital to the health and success of post-Civil War America.

This book answers the question of why these three figures should be remembered as three of the most prominent civil rights leaders in history as they are among the first U.S. politicians to use their political power in the interest of black rights. There were of course other leaders who advocated for the civil rights, or basic legal rights, of African Americans. However, unlike other civil rights advocates, Stevens, Grant, and Sumner fought to give African Americans more than just basic civil rights, but social equality in the public sphere. In the subsequent chapters, I outlined events from their early years that explain why these men developed a moral obligation for black equality and then analyze a specific piece of civil rights legislation that each was responsible for creating, developing, or was extremely influential in its passage. Finally, using a mixture of secondary sources from historians and primary documents from the time period, I have portrayed how each was of important and of legendary stature in the era that they lived. This analysis takes place through separate sections for each man, organized by the chronology of the legislation that each influenced. However, first, a basic understanding of Reconstruction, dubbed by historians as the "most controversial chapter in our history," is necessary. Combined with a brief analysis of the constantly evolving historiography, the introduction section helps explain why I feel the achievements of Thaddeus Stevens, Ulysses S. Grant, and Charles Sumner need to be reexamined in the context of civil rights.[4]

chapter one

INTRODUCTION

A Brief Political Overview of Reconstruction

Following Robert E. Lee's surrender at Appomattox Court House on April 9, 1865, the Civil War had officially come to a close. However, the nation became flooded with an array of problems following the conclusion of the bloodiest war in American history; thus, how would President Abraham Lincoln reconcile the goals of the war? At the beginning of Lincoln's second term, he needed to figure out a way to deal with Southern states and ex-Confederates, integrate millions of ex-slaves into the country, and most of all, reunite a country that had been at war for the last four years. The main themes of reunion and emancipation were gigantic problems that had no historical precedent in the United States. However, only a few months into his term, Lincoln was shot and killed, leaving Andrew Johnson with the responsibility of reuniting this extremely fractured nation.

The Reconstruction era, 1865-1877, can be divided up into two opposite political movements: Presidential Reconstruction and Radical (or Congressional) Reconstruction. Upon taking office, President Johnson immediately—and a bit surprisingly—veered away from Abraham Lincoln's Reconstruction plan of gradually allowing ex-Confederate States back in the Union. Instead, Johnson quickly issued a proclamation of amnesty and pardon to the Southern elite and ex-Confederates.[1] As a result, Johnson became a champion of the white man, provided little punishment for ex-Confederates, and created a blueprint for Presidential Reconstruction that included "no commitment to civil equality" for freedmen.[2] Although Southern whites were prepared to accept any punishments handed out by the government and possibly even black suffrage, Presiden-

6

tial Reconstruction offered the stark opposite; Johnson appointed mostly pro-Confederates to governorships and other political positions in Southern States as well as thousands of pardons to ex-Confederates.[3] Thus, Johnson's policies under Presidential Reconstruction "failed to create a new political leadership to replace the prewar 'slaveocracy,'" Eric Foner wrote, "partly because the President himself so quickly aligned with portions of the old elite."[4] Despite the passage of the Thirteenth Amendment officially outlawing slavery in 1865, the new President had reversed the Reconstruction theme of emancipation. Andrew Johnson's Reconstruction plan allowed for Southern lawmakers to enact the "Black Codes;" local laws aimed to oppress the freedmen in discriminatory labor laws as well as heavy taxes and limited access to resources. Overall, Presidential Reconstruction had actually "introduced the whole pattern of disenfranchisement, discrimination, and segregation into the postwar South."[5]

Through Johnson's anti-Freedpeople stance and his leniency toward ex-Confederates, the Republicans in Congress became upset with his policies and Reconstruction plan; leaders such as Charles Sumner and Thaddeus Stevens both aggressively pushed for full equality for blacks and ridiculed the President for taking the country back to its prewar state. Though Republicans were initially hesitant to break away from Johnson, "northern voters turned to the Republicans and gave them a mandate to try a reconstruction plan of their own."[6] With a large Republican majority in office following the election of 1866, Radical (or Congressional) Reconstruction had begun. Charles Sumner and Thaddeus Stevens—the unofficial leaders in the Senate and House, respectively—were two of the most influential proponents who helped rescind Johnson's previous policies and began securing a civil rights movement for

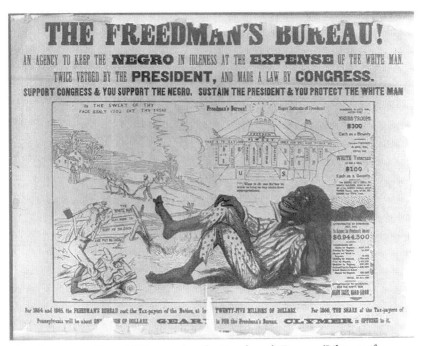

A racist cartoon from 1866 smearing the Freedman's Bureau (Library of Congress)

African Americans. Radical Republicans in Congress, given the name because of their progressive stance on black rights, immediately terminated the Black Codes and created the Freedman's Bureau in 1865 as a way to provide economic assistance to blacks.[7] Despite President Johnson's stark opposition to almost every bill that the Republicans proposed, Republicans passed an array of civil rights legislation as part of their "civic ideology."[8] For the first time in America's political discourse, black equality was at the forefront of a major party's platform. With this focus, Republicans overrode both of President Johnson's vetoes to pass the Civil Rights Act of 1866 and the Fourteenth Amendment a year later.[9] The years of 1865 and 1866 produced unprecedented legislative control by one party, as the Republicans even attempted to impeach Andrew Johnson for "high crimes and misdemeanors" and for the removal of Secretary of War Edwin Stanton (or more accurately for disagreeing with their policies), falling short of conviction by one vote.[10]

In 1867, the final phase of Congressional Reconstruction occurred with the passage of four Reconstruction Acts which divided ten of the eleven Confederate states (Tennessee being the exception) into "five military districts under commanders empowered to employ the army to protect life and property."[11] These acts had a considerable effect on Southern states; not only did they declare that states must ratify the Fourteenth Amendment to regain admission to the Union, but they allowed military officers to protect the rights of blacks in Southern states and legally discriminate against ex-Confederates in the voting booth.[12] Furthermore, former Union General Ulysses S. Grant, a Republican, won the election of 1868 and only a year later aided the passage of the Fifteenth Amendment into the Constitution, which granted black male suffrage. For the next four years, the Grant Administration and the remaining Radical Republicans in Congress continued their focus on the themes of Reconstruction: emancipation and reunion. Due to the aforementioned laws that had recently been passed, the economic fortunes of African Americans improved as government attempted to protect them from the vitriol and violence in the South—which they did with varying levels of success and failure.[13] Furthermore, blacks had success at the voting booth, gaining representation in government at both the state and national level. However, by 1871, the "prospect of continued Republican control of all branches of the government was dimmed"; politically, the country was still extremely split as the power began to shift to the Democrats.[14] Historians Allan Nevins and Henry S. Commager argued that since Republicanism "became identified with the notion of racial equality—a notion intolerable to most Southerners at the time," it was those "ill-advised politics" that weakened the Republican Party instead of strengthening it.[15] Although President Grant was re-elected in 1872 and many African Americans enjoyed various civil rights that they would not again have until the mid-twentieth century, many governorships fell into Democratic hands as the Ku Klux Klan and other white supremacist groups became "deeply entrenched in nearly every Southern state."[16] Following the election of 1876, Reconstruction came to an end as the progressive changes in America were quickly undone.

Rutherford B. Hayes, a Republican, won the presidency over Democrat Samuel Tilden by one Electoral College vote in the highly disputed election of 1876; however, as a compromise with the Democrats, Hayes promised as president to withdraw the remaining federal troops in the South.[17] Therefore, without military protection in the southern states, blacks were relegated back to second-class citizens with little protection under the law. By 1877, Reconstruction—the attempted effort to reunite the country and secure civil rights for blacks—had officially come to a close.

The Historiography

The controversial historiography of Reconstruction can initially be traced back to the "Lost Cause," in which various groups following the Civil War attempted to reframe the Confederate cause as noble. In addition, "Lost Cause" supporters condemned the Union and framed Reconstruction as a tragic era that, ironically, erased black gains. Historian James McPherson wrote that, "Confederate veterans felt an ever greater need to enshrine their deeds in stone or bronze and inspire future generations with the nobility of their cause."[18] Groups

A United Confederate Veterans reunion in North Carolina in 1917 (Library of Congress)

such as the United Confederate Veterans, United Daughters of the Confederacy, and the Sons of Confederate Veterans escalated this "Lost Cause" mentality in the subsequent years.

The so-called "Dunning School," led by William Dunning, a Professor of Political Philosophy at Columbia University, was responsible for the expansion of the "Lost Cause" interpretations of Reconstruction in the early 1900s. Dunning and his graduate students, who also became widely respected scholars, published essays and books condemning Reconstruction as "the darkest page in the saga of American history."[19] Dunning contemporary and Columbia colleague John W. Burgess called Reconstruction, "the most soul-sickening spectacle that Americans had ever been called upon to behold."[20] Historian Eric Foner summed up the Dunning School view very succinctly: Dunning, Foner argued, interpreted Reconstruction as a time when the white South "genuinely accepted the reality of military defeat" and was ready to participate in Reconstruction until the Radical Republicans hijacked Congress. Dunning claimed that the Radical Republicans were "motivated by an irrational hatred of Southern 'rebels,' led by nasty 'carpetbaggers' and 'ignorant freedman' who forced the country into an 'era of corruption.'"[21] Dunning referred to blacks as the "ignorant many" as his "racial bias was unquestionably present in all of Dunning's own books on Reconstruction..."[22] Dunning contemporary and black scholar W.E.B. DuBois wrote that,

> Not a single great leader of the nation during the Civil War and Reconstruction has escaped attack and libel. The magnificent figures of Charles Sumner and Thaddeus Stevens have been besmirched almost beyond recognition. We have been cajoling and flattering the South and slurring the North...[23]

However, what remains important to understand is not necessarily explaining the detailed synopsis of the Dunning School's view, but the depiction on how his interpretation of Reconstruction became so ingrained in American society until the late 1960s. Historiographer Frances FitzGerald argued that this is the version of Reconstruction that most adults grew up understanding as history texts during the first half of the century included a "passionate defense" of President Andrew Johnson, intense criticism of the "harsh, vindictive Thaddeus Stevens" and the idea that "Radical Reconstruction was an unmitigated disaster."[24] This negative portrayal was held in textbooks all throughout the country. Historian Kyle Ward, who had compared textbooks throughout the last three decades agreed that, "the textbook becomes an essential part of how U.S. students learn about their past."[25] For example, Ward explained how U.S. history textbooks in the early twentieth century "helped develop the racist mythology of the Reconstruction era" and how textbooks still adhered "closely to the racist version of U.S. history" during the 1930s.[26] Even more, Ward gave an example of a U.S. history textbook from 1950 that remarkably kept the Dunning narrative of Reconstruction intact.[27] Changing the deeply flawed view of Reconstruction would not be an easy task to accomplish.

Eric Foner explained that, "despite its remarkable longevity and powerful hold on the popular imagination, the demise of the traditional interpretation was inevitable."[28] Despite much of American history being rewritten during the late 1960s, Reconstruction emerged as the most dramatically revised period of all; Frances Fitz-Gerald described this new interpretation as a "total inversion" from the previously adhered to views.[29] Instead, by the late 1960s Reconstruction was portrayed more positively, with new texts claiming Andrew Johnson lacked "dignity and judgment, and concern for the rights of the freedman" and that "the courageous Thaddeus Stevens" stood up against him.[30] This view was a direct opposite of the aforementioned traditionalist view. In sharp contrast from the malevolent era portrayed by "Lost Cause" supporters, historians on the political left came up "with a striking new thesis that the Radical Republicans had not gone far enough [to securing black rights]..."[31] Foner added that, "the 1960s revisionist wave broke over the field, destroying in rapid succession, every assumption of the traditional viewpoint."[32] In addition, the period of the 1960s promoted a progressive political atmosphere that aided revisionists' belief that Reconstruction was a time that should be commended for its achievements, even if they were limited in scope. Instead of "rampant misgovernment" by the Radical Republicans, they instead directed "a time of extraordinary social and political progress for blacks."[33] This new revisionist thesis—in stark opposition to the traditionalist view—completely recast Reconstruction in a new light for over twenty years until the story of Reconstruction evolved yet again with the addition of recent scholarship.

In the course of about ten years during the 1960s, the interpretation of Reconstruction had evolved from a tragic and corrupt era in American history to a time of significant and unparalleled achievements. However, modern scholarship has now attempted to revisit the revisionist view and ask whether Reconstruction was really a time of such radical change.[34] Recently, postrevisionists—while completely discrediting the blatant racism in the traditional interpretation—have tried to find a middle ground between the two opposing perspectives. How radical really were the years of Reconstruction? Historians such as C. Vann Woodward claimed Reconstruction was actually a relatively conservative time in terms of changes, yet Foner contended that such a view holds little merit when it "took the nation fully a century to implement its most basic demands [of civil rights]..."[35] Most importantly, postrevisionists have attempted to re-evaluate Reconstruction in a broader context and in a politically neutral climate. Foner again argued that, "historians have yet to produce a coherent account of Reconstruction," a reason why he wrote his most recent account that may be the first to effectively do so.[36]

Reframing Reconstruction

In general, the most widely accepted view of Reconstruction admitted that although corruption undoubtedly occurred and blacks never achieved the economic freedom they had hoped, Reconstruction was a positive, progressive time in American history that gave blacks many civil rights that they would not possess again until almost a century later. Through this complex evolution, African Americans have now become the center of the Reconstruction debate producing a subtle, but different, kind of distortion. Understanding the civil rights gains that African Americans secured through the passages of the Thirteenth, Fourteenth, and Fifteenth Amendments have defined the Reconstruction Era. In result of all these historical revisions and interpretations, Reconstruction history had produced a view that was solely focused on social history from the "bottom up."[37] In effect, these revisions that zeroed in on Reconstruction's social history—and solely began to focus on blacks—had prevented some of the Era's most important and charismatic figures from receiving the recognition that so many other figures in America have received. The Reconstruction Amendments are extremely important and extraordinary, yet, it is important to not forget *how* they were passed and the *people* who made them pass.

While looking at history from ordinary people's perspectives such as Southern blacks or Northern working whites gives us a good framework of the time period, it is important to realize who actually held the tangible power during these years. For example, while people such as Frederick Douglass were extremely important to the civil rights movement during Reconstruction, he held little actual legislative power; for blacks to realistically gain the freedom they deserved—and that he so eloquently orated about—there had to be substantial leaders in government willing to fight for black equality. Legislative and lawmaking power was located at the top of the political system as the people who held these positions—and actually created the progressive policies of Reconstruction—had been 'lost in translation' through the constant revisions of Reconstruction's social history. While historians had attempted to straighten out the facts of Reconstruction, erase the biases of previous views and more recently, create one coherent narrative, this positive scholarship had inadvertently done some harm; somehow, Reconstruction's evolution allowed for extremely popular figures and famous—or infamous—people during Reconstruction to be effectively erased from American history books.[38]

The on-going revisions on Reconstruction had emphasized the social history of this era, too often only relying on African American figures—and unintentionally leaving out the critical political figures that legislated the remarkable political, social, and economic changes. This book seeks to offer insight and analysis into three of the most important political figures from the Reconstruction Age—President U.S. Grant, Massachusetts Senator Charles Sumner, and Pennsylvania Congressman Thaddeus Stevens—whose contributions will be examined once again in the ongoing re-evaluation of this vastly important time period. The recognition that these men deserve based on their achievements has somehow eluded them as they are—at least in part—largely responsible for many of the positive gains of Reconstruction concerning civil rights. There remains no doubt that without the dedication, commitment, and passion that each man displayed towards securing the civil rights of African Americans in an extremely prejudiced and politically turbulent time period, future civil rights progress in the 1960s would not have happened the way it did. It is my hope that through this book the deeds, triumphs, and sacrifices that these three great, yet very imperfect, men made towards securing civil rights in America will not only garner larger attention, but eventually be included in history textbooks and credited as the first civil rights leaders in the first American Civil Rights Movement. Every era produced its great figures: Revolutionary America—George Washington and Thomas Jefferson, Antebellum America—Henry Clay and Daniel Webster, Civil War America—Abraham Lincoln, World

INTRODUCTION

War II America–Franklin Roosevelt, and Civil Rights America—Martin Luther King, Jr. Frankly, Americans must be reminded about other great figures who also contributed to the progress of this country; Americans need to recognize Thaddeus Stevens, Ulysses S. Grant, and Charles Sumner as great "civil rights" leaders who were at the forefront of America's First Civil Rights Movement during Reconstruction.

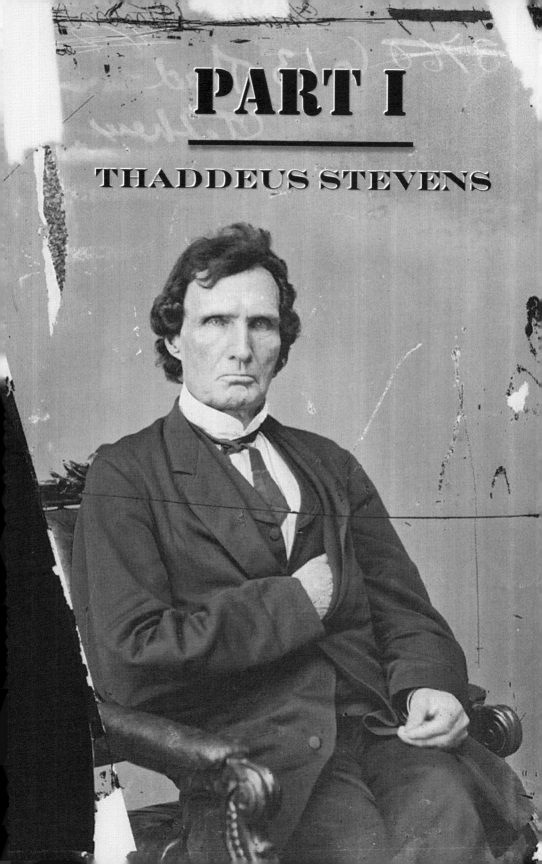

PART I

THADDEUS STEVENS

Fourteenth Amendment of the Constitution of the United States of America

Section 1. All persons born or naturalized in the United States, and subject to the jurisdiction thereof, are citizens of the United States and of the State wherein they reside. No State shall make or enforce any law which shall abridge the privileges or immunities of citizens of the United States; nor shall any State deprive any person of life, liberty, or property, without due process of law; nor deny to any person within its jurisdiction the equal protection of the laws.

Section 2. Representatives shall be apportioned among the several States according to their respective numbers, counting the whole number of persons in each State, excluding Indians not taxed. But when the right to vote at any election for the choice of electors for President and Vice President of the United States, Representatives in Congress, the Executive and Judicial officers of a State, or the members of the Legislature thereof, is denied to any of the male inhabitants of such State, being twenty-one years of age, and citizens of the United States, or in any way abridged, except for participation in rebellion, or other crime, the basis of representation therein shall be reduced in the proportion which the number of such male citizens shall bear to the whole number of male citizens twenty-one years of age in such State.

Section 3. No person shall be a Senator or Representative in Congress, or elector of President and Vice President, or hold any office, civil or military, under the United States, or under any State, who, having previously taken an oath, as a member of Congress, or as an officer of the United States, or as a member of any State legislature, or as an executive or judicial officer of any State, to support the Constitution of the United States, shall have engaged in insurrection or rebellion against the same, or given aid or comfort to the enemies thereof. But Congress may, by a vote of two-thirds of each House, remove such disability.

Section 4. The validity of the public debt of the United States, authorized by law, including debts incurred for payment of pensions and bounties for services in suppressing insurrection or rebellion, shall not be questioned. But neither the United States nor any State shall assume or pay any debt or obligation incurred in aid of insurrection or rebellion against the United States, or any claim for the loss or emancipation of any slave; but all such debts, obligations and claims shall be held illegal and void.

Section 5. The Congress shall have power to enforce, by appropriate legislation, the provisions of this article.

HARPER'S WEEKLY.

A JOURNAL OF CIVILIZATION

chapter two

THE CREATION OF AN ADVOCATE

" *Strange as it may sound to American ears, the course of liberty is hard to sustain in this republic.* "

– Thaddeus Stevens, 1850

In D.W. Griffith's famous 1914 film *Birth of a Nation*, Thaddeus Stevens, one of the main characters, was portrayed as a highly corrupt man who had a deep seated hatred for white people and negatively influenced Southern legislatures. This "misleading and historically wrong" depiction of Stevens heavily tarnished his legacy; *Birth of a Nation* had generated over fifty million dollars in revenue and became one of the most successful movies in history.[1] At the time, the "Lost Cause" perspective of Reconstruction still reigned supreme and despite some outspoken critics to the movie, Americans generally grew up with the idea of the monstrous Thaddeus Stevens. Although he was cast in such a negative light, Director D.W. Griffith chose Stevens because of his undeniably important and recognizable role in Reconstruction.

Modern historical scholarship has corrected the view of Thaddeus Stevens, pointing out that he was a man of deep moral principles and one of the preeminent supporters of equal rights for blacks. However, what has seemingly disappeared in the process of historical revision is, well, Thaddeus Stevens himself; "if one mentions Thaddeus Stevens to the average American one is likely to receive a questioning look," argued historian Ralph Korngold, and "few have ever heard of him."[2] Despite his firm place among historians, his name holds minimal significance in the public sphere. During his lifetime, Stevens was extremely influential and in many ways, the father of civil rights. As a Congressman in his early seventies from 1859-1868, Stevens was well known for his fiery and compassionate speeches against the oppressive state of race relations. The unquestioned leader of House Republicans, "Stevens was a master of Congressional infighting, parliamentary tactics, and blunt speaking."[3] Even those who disagreed with his then-radical opinions on equal rights "could not avoid a grudging admiration for the man and his honesty, idealism, and indifference to praise and criticism—qualities not altogether common among politicians."[4] Ultimately, Stevens' greatest accomplishment was the Fourteenth Amendment; the Congressman helped draft the original Amendment and also had a prominent role in its passage. However, an initial context of a few selected events in his early years is essential to understanding Thaddeus Stevens' moral conscience for pursuing civil rights.

The Early Years

Stevens was born in 1792 into a poor family in Danville, Vermont.[5] It was for this reason that Carter G. Woodson, the founder of black history, wrote that, "he sympathized with the man far down."[6] Not only did he grow up impoverished but he was born with a clubfoot. Stevens struggled to fit in with his deformity, often on the defensive, as "his wit became a formidable weapon and, what he lacked in physical dexterity he more than made up for in verbal skill."[7] His fierce oratorical skills that he developed at a young age would define him as a politician in future years. Yet, his clubfoot continued to haunt him throughout his entire life. In addition, at age 39, Stevens went permanently bald due to an apparent attack of typhoid fever, which left him using a wig for the remainder of his life. Ultimately, his physical insecurities most likely played a role in why he never married and had reportedly very few mistresses. However, one mistress, Lydia Hamilton Smith, an African American of mixed racial descent, later moved into a cottage behind Stevens' house in 1848 to help him take care of his nephews. Eventually, "Mrs. Smith," as she was spoken of in great dignity—"a regard rarely shown to Negroes in that day"— moved to Stevens' main house and lived there until his death. Rumors of their intimacy plagued him throughout his career, though Stevens consistently denied it and no document had ever proved otherwise.[8]

Pushing aside personal struggles, Stevens graduated from Dartmouth College in 1814, with a commencement speech in which he declared, "unequal distribution of wealth was necessary to progress."[9] Stevens was a strong believer in free enterprise and became a successful businessman outside of his political career, owning three ironworks in Gettysburg.[10] His belief in a considerably free-labor ideology advanced his progressive perspective on civil rights; he passionately believed in equal opportunity and that privilege based on uncontrollable factors, especially race, must be fully eradicated from American society. Following graduation, Stevens was offered a teaching position in Pennsylvania before eventually pursuing a more lucrative career as a lawyer. Through a variety of successful yet controversial trials, he became one of the top lawyers in Pennsylvania.

Yet, as historian and Stevens biographer Fawn Brodie noted, it was his first case that seemed "to have been critical in Stevens' life, for it thrust him headlong into a labyrinth he was never afterward to escape—the Negro problem."[11] In this case in 1821, Stevens, who was beginning to earn a name for himself as a prominent lawyer, defended—successfully—a slaveholder in court who looked to regain the possession of his slave.[12] However, this would not be how Stevens would be remembered; Stevens would vigorously fight on blacks' behalf for the rest of his life and punished himself dearly for what he had done.[13] Out of guilt, anguish, regret or all of the above, his defense of "the victory seems to have been ashes in his mouth...this slave whose hopes of freedom he had smashed, apparently taught the twenty-nine-year-old lawyer something he had not learned in books—that the law can be an instrument of terror as well as justice."[14] Just two years later in 1823, Stevens proclaimed at a public Fourth of July dinner, "may he [the next president] be a freeman, who never riveted fetters on a human slave."[15] Stevens' public tirade against slavery had begun even though holding such a viewpoint was dangerous in southern Pennsylvania in 1823 because despite the abolishment of slavery in the north, most whites still held deep prejudices towards blacks.[16]

Another anecdote deserves mention in framing the character and career of Thaddeus Stevens. With his law practice beginning to grow in Gettysburg, Pennsylvania, Stevens desperately needed to buy additional law books. Therefore, Stevens took three hundred dollars and rode to Baltimore on horseback where during his journey, he heard an enslaved woman crying in the hall of the inn at which he resided. Stevens went to see who was in despair, and in between sobs the woman explained that her husband, also enslaved, was about to be sold. Upon hearing this, Stevens went up to the proprietor who was buying the woman's husband and offered to buy the slave for one hundred and fifty dollars, screaming "aren't you ashamed to sell your own flesh and blood?" Failing to recognize the barbarity of his actions, the proprietor responded that the slave would cost three hundred dollars. In response, Stevens "put down the money, manumitted the slave, and rode home without the coveted law books."[17] This story hinted at the growing moral awareness that Stevens was developing; he had ridden for days just to buy law books and yet, despite it being a large inconvenience and significant financial sacrifice, Stevens could not bear to watch a slave suffer, freeing him without hesitation.

In the late 1820s, while continuing his law practice, Stevens began to dabble in politics before becoming highly involved in the local Anti-Masonic party.[18] His passionate crusades against Freemasonry—whether due to his own insecurities or just because of his political ambi-

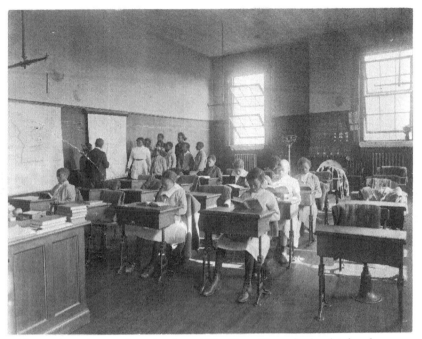

African American students in class at Thaddeus Stevens' school, taken between 1900 and 1920 (Library of Congress)

tions—helped Stevens gain local prominence and was successfully elected to the Pennsylvania State Legislature in 1830. Stevens quickly rose in the world of state politics, mastering "parliamentary law" and became a "guiding force of his party."[19] By 1834, Stevens' intense crusade against Masonry as well as his advocacy for public education continued to generate attention. The latter issue would become one of his greatest passions; a speech he made in the state legislature reportedly reversed a bill denouncing public education and instead, it passed as he took "great pride in his reputation as the father of free education in Pennsylvania."[20] As a state legislator, Stevens had also expressed early in his career that slavery was wrong; in 1835 he attempted—although it failed—to pass a resolution to encourage the termination of slavery even though he knew the North possessed little power to interfere with Southern states. Stevens believed that "the ownership of human beings was wrong and that equal rights were the cornerstone of republican institutions."[21] However it was not until 1837 that he went public with this message as he declared at the Pennsylvania Constitutional Convention in July that, "the domestic slavery of this country was the most disgraceful institution that the world had ever witnessed, under any form of Government, in any age." The records of the Constitutional Convention also state that Stevens wished he "were the owner of every Southern slave, so that I might cast off the shackles from their limbs, and witness the rapture which would excite them in their first dance of their freedom."[22] Sent to the Convention to help reframe the State Constitution, Stevens became so unhappy with the statutes denying blacks voting rights that by the end of the Convention he refused to even sign the document.[23]

By this time, Stevens became one of the prominent politicians in Pennsylvania due partially to his political savvy. The other part of his success lay in his amazing oratory skills that would later captivate the House of Representatives during discussions on civil rights. He continued to fight passionately against the Fugitive Slave Law but frustrated with the lack of success, temporarily left politics after his final term in the Pennsylvania Legislature in 1842. From 1842 to 1849, Stevens returned to his law career, in which he "gained a reputation for defending those who harbored fugitive slaves."[24] During these years, Stevens had stayed away from politics, although his rage about the extension of slavery kept him interested in national affairs. As a result, the Whig Party nominated him for National Congress in 1849 where he won the election.[25] During his four years as a Congressman, Stevens immediately established himself as a leading abolitionist, viciously attacking the Fugitive Slave Law, which he thought was absolutely despicable. During a discussion of the law on the House floor, Stevens compared slavery to the Biblical story of the Great Plague in Egypt, describing the country as a "land of wicked slavery." Stevens then declared:

> I will never consent to the admission of another slave State in the Union on account of the injustice of slave representation...There are twenty-five representatives on this floor who are virtually the representatives of slaves alone, having not one free constituent. This is an *outrage* on every representative principle...[26]

Stevens, despite being a newcomer in Washington, D.C., had risen to become a leading anti-slavery figure; a long list of State and National Senators and Representatives had sent Stevens and others a letter stating that they were, "highly approving of your course in Congress on the slavery question and regarding with admiration your manly truthful and eloquent opposition to the usurpations of slavery..."[27] Yet, due to a race riot in Lancaster following the passage of the Fugitive Slave Law in 1850, Stevens' support of the law and of civil rights resulted in a failure to be re-elected in 1853 as he believed that his political career had ended.[28] However, with the passage of the Kansas-Nebraska Act in 1854, which threatened to have Kansas enter the Union as a slave state, Stevens once again became politically active in 1855; the extension of slavery resulted in the creation of the Republican Party whose platform solely centered on the protest of slavery.[29] Therefore, Stevens immediately joined the anti-slavery Republican Party as they "won a gifted politician who could be counted on to pursue the party ideals with a frightening intensity."[30] Although Stevens continued his lucrative law career during his political hiatus, he remained a staunch abolitionist who "never relinquished his determination to use all political means available to stop the spread of slavery."[31] Stevens ran one more time for Congress—successfully—as a Republican in 1859. At the age of 68, the stage was set for Thaddeus Stevens to become one of America's forefathers of civil rights legislation.

Following the breakout of the Civil War, Stevens immediately was one of the most outspoken radical proponents for the Union cause. In addition to Charles Sumner in the Senate, he had become the leader of the so-called "Radical Republicans," an anti-slavery group whose agenda was to end slavery and punish the South—by any means necessary.[32] Throughout the early stages of the war, the only issue that mattered for Stevens was ending slavery; in fact, emancipation, one of the big themes of Reconstruction in subsequent years, became an obsession. Fawn Brodie wrote that, "Stevens had one touchstone by which he tested his superiors and supported or abandoned his friends—the vigor with

A Harper's Weekly Magazine illustrating the scene of the House floor following the passage of the Thirteenth Amendment in 1865 (Library of Congress)

which they moved in the antislavery cause."[33] Stevens became a "radical of radicals," willing to do whatever was necessary to win the war and abolish slavery at any cost, "always goading the president" to emancipate the slaves.[34] However, very few Republicans were as radical as Stevens because while many Republicans supported emancipation, they did so only as a means to save the Union. In comparison, Stevens barred no racial prejudice and supported emancipation not just to secure a Union victory, but because slavery was "the most hateful and infernal blot that ever disgraced the escutcheon of man..."[35]

When the Union officially won the Civil War on April 9, 1865, eight months later the passage of the Thirteenth Amendment—the abolition of slavery—would bring "crowning triumph" as Stevens entered the final years of his life with more vigor than ever to fight for the rights of freedmen. However, Stevens and the other Radicals in Congress were well aware of how incomplete the Amendment was; the Thirteenth Amendment merely outlawed slavery while every type of discrimination toward African Americans remained legal. The Pennsylvania Congressman understood that an additional Amendment that would protect the rights of millions of vulnerable new freedpeople was an urgent necessity—in result, when Congress resumed in 1866, Thaddeus Stevens immediately began drafting the Fourteenth Amendment.

chapter three

THE FIGHT FOR THE 14TH AMENDMENT

"From this rebellion the Republic will emerge reunited, purified, strengthened, and glorious through all time; or it will sink into profound despotism, slavery, and infamy."

\- Thaddeus Stevens, 1866

With the abolishment of slavery by the Thirteenth Amendment and four million ex-slaves now free, the drama of trying to reconcile the nation back together had begun. Stevens made the transition from staunch abolitionist during the Civil War to unquestioned leader for black rights during the commencement of the 39th Congress. Contemporary historian William H. Barnes wrote that, "It was a fitting reward that he, in 1866, should stand in the United States House of Representatives, at the head of a majority of more than one hundred, declaring that the oppressed race should enjoy rights so long denied."[1] Thaddeus Stevens was at the forefront of the anti-slavery movement prior to the war and upon its conclusion, made it his mission to secure emancipation—a main pillar of the Union cause—and create equal rights for blacks. Historian Hans Trefousse agreed that, "Stevens' prominence in Congress was widely recognized."[2]

While Stevens did not agree with Lincoln's generous Ten-Percent Plan of lightly punishing the South, the assassination of President Lincoln in April of 1865 significantly affected Stevens and the Radical Republicans' plan for civil rights.[3] President Andrew Johnson, who ascended to the Presidency following Lincoln's assassination, conversely believed in pardoning ex-Confederates and denying the rights of African Americans. However, black rights had already soared to the top of the Republican agenda and after a bitter fight between the Radical Republicans in Congress and President Johnson, the Republican majority overrode Johnson's veto to pass the Civil Rights Act of 1866—the first of its kind. Despite Stevens' work on getting the Civil Rights Bill passed, he knew that any law could be repealed by a majority or declared unconstitutional.[4] Stevens wanted to make sure these civil rights gains would be permanent and therefore, with the help of former Indiana Congressman Robert Dale Owen, drafted a

A racist poster created as part of a smear campaign by Democrats, drawn in 1866 (Library of Congress)

single constitutional amendment to give to the Joint Committee on Reconstruction.[5] Brodie contended that Stevens issued great influence on writing this document, which would eventually become the Fourteenth Amendment.[6] He would spend the next two years fighting aggressively for the passage and ratification of one of the most important Amendments in history.

In January 1866, Stevens gave a passionate speech during an initial proposal of the Fourteenth Amendment expressing his extreme hatred for pro-slavery advocates. Fully grasping the significance of future decisions, Stevens exclaimed that African Americans were either going to be "treated as our fathers declared by solemn declaration they ought to be treated, or to be oppressed by us as insolent tyrants, by which we will deserve the execrations of the human race." Stevens understood that the decisions of this time period would impact the country forever and further added that, "the time has come when we can make the Constitution what our fathers desired to make it...the time has come when through blood every stain has been washed out unless we choose to reestablish it."[7]

The biggest internal quandary for Stevens was not just the prejudice that existed in the country, but understanding how the rights of freedmen fit into the definition of the Republic. In his initial proposal, suffrage rights were included as he stated in front of the House floor that, "this proposition [suffrage and equal rights] rests upon a principle already imbedded in the Constitution, and as old as free government itself..." Stevens continued that the Amendment would enforce the true principles of this country by affording civil rights and suffrage.[8]

However, once his proposal came back from the Committee, Stevens was outraged; while the provisions from the Civil Rights Act of 1866 that prohibited racial discrimination were included, the provision on Negro suffrage had been stripped.[9] Stevens had already stated his position a few months earlier criticizing those who opposed suffrage. Stevens mocked that, "the whole copperhead party, pandering to the lowest prejudices of the ignorant, repeat the cuckoo cry, "This is a white man's Government..."" Stevens continued by asking:

> What is implied by this? That one race of men are to have the exclusive right forever to rule this nation, and to exercise all acts of sovereignty, while all other races and nations and colors are to be their subjects, and have no voice in making the laws and choosing the rulers by whom they are to be governed. Wherein does this differ from slavery except in degree?[10]

Stevens further believed that, the "equal rights to all the privileges of the Government is innate in every immortal being, no matter what the shape or color of the tabernacle which it inhabits."[11] Therefore, when the Fourteenth Amendment proposal did not include suffrage for former slaves, Stevens criticized the cowardice of his party members who worried about the political consequences of including the suffrage provision.[12] Yet, Stevens understood the hostile political atmosphere in that he "subordinated his dreams for a political paradise—and also his hatred of the Southern white—to the necessities of practical politics."[13] With the first official draft of the Fourteenth Amendment on the table, Stevens worked tirelessly and did whatever was necessary to pass the critical vote. Under Congressional Reconstruction, while Southern states were required to ratify the Amendment to gain entry intro the Union, Stevens took full responsibility for getting it to that stage. In doing that, Stevens put his political principles towards civil rights above his friends and other colleagues; he felt that "the most exemplary personal behavior or moral rectitude meant nothing if a man's voting record was anti-Negro."[14]

An undated portrait sketch of Stevens
(Library of Congress)

Combined with other measures, the Fourteenth Amendment was supposed to secure citizenship and protect the basic civil rights of African Americans. Among all Congressmen, no public servant was more passionate, dedicated, or so one-dimensionally committed to this cause than Stevens. In early May, Stevens directly addressed how important the Fourteenth Amendment was in fulfilling the principles of the Declaration of Independence; after reading the first equal protection clause section to his colleagues, Stevens declared that, "I can hardly believe that any person can be found who will not admit that every one of these provisions is just."[15] Still, it was not lost upon Stevens that the Fourteenth Amendment did not provide everything that he originally drafted months before; Stevens admitted that his original draft sent to the Senate secured more rights. Even though he supported the Amendment in its current form, Stevens made it known that "we shall not approach the measure of justice until we have given every adult freedman a homestead on the land where he was born and toiled and suffered."[16] Putting it in perspective, Stevens was ahead of his time; he fully understood the magnitude of slavery as an oppressive, inhumane institution. While there were other Radical Republicans who supported civil rights—each to varying degrees—none put their career and life on the line like Thaddeus Stevens or better understood the hypocrisy of both the Constitution and Declaration of Independence.

With the release of the final version of the Fourteenth Amendment, the actual document was "a far less tough and exacting document than Thaddeus Stevens had hoped for."[17] The Fourteenth Amendment stated that the right to vote, "…denied to any of the male inhabitants of such State, being twenty-one years of age, and citizens of the United States, or in any way abridged, except for participation in rebellion, or other crime, the basis of representation therein shall be reduced in the proportion which the number of such male citizens shall bear to the whole number of male citizens twenty-one years of age in such State."[18] To the disappointment of Stevens, the Amendment did not bar voting discrimination on the basis of race or previous servitude as Stevens regretfully declared that:

> ...I have fondly dreamed that when any fortunate chance could have broken up for awhile the foundation of our institutions, and released us from obligations the most tyrannical that man ever imposed in the name of freedom, that the intelligent, pure and just men of this Republic, true to their professions and their conscience, would have so remodeled all our institutions as to have freed them from every vestige of human oppression, of inequality of rights, of the recognized degradation of the poor, and the superior caste of the rich....This bright dream has vanished 'like a baseless fabric of a vision.'[19]

Overall, while the Fourteenth Amendment did not secure all the rights that Stevens had hoped for, it made permanent the Civil Rights Act of 1866 while expanding citizenship for African American males. Constitutional lawyer Michael J. Perry further argued that, "the due process and equal protection provisions... were understood to communicate norms that transcend the historical circumstance that occasioned the Fourteenth Amendment."[20] Furthermore, in terms of present day importance, the civil rights issues that Stevens and the other Radical Republicans dealt with were "a microcosm of those that impact the development of constitutional law more generally," today.[21] Frankly, the passage and ratification of the Fourteenth Amendment was an extremely important and symbolic event in the progress of black rights. Law Professor Earl M. Waltz agreed that the Fourteenth Amendment, "introduced a novel concept into mainstream constitutional jurisprudence—the idea that racial discrimination was per se suspect," or on an individual basis.[22] Most importantly, Thaddeus Stevens' role in securing this landmark Amendment was absolutely critical; he was the first to push the initial idea for an

Amendment, helped draft the legislation, and fought strongly for its passage as the leader of Congress. For Stevens, the passage of the Fourteenth Amendment was intended to be another permanent step to the freedmen's "new birth of freedom."[23]

chapter four
OLD THAD STEVENS REMEMBERED

" I will be satisfied if my epitaph shall be written thus: ' Here lies one who never rose to any eminence, and who only courted the low ambition to have it said that he had striven to ame- liorate the condition of the poor, the lowly, the downtrodden of every race and language and color.'"

— Thaddeus Stevens, 1866

For the few remaining months of his life, Stevens continued to fight for black rights and played a key role in creating the Reconstruction Act of 1867 that paved way for the five military districts that would govern the South. Stevens' dramatic speech in support of the bill "in a voice so weak his colleagues had to crowd around him," notably helped the bill pass.[1] While the idea of having military intervention may not have been a good measure, Stevens' justification was not only that he wanted to punish the South, but more importantly, that there was still "so much to be accomplished" in terms of civil rights.[2] In addition, Stevens also wanted to increase the allotment of land for freedman and especially, put forth a public education bill. Days before his passing, Stevens stated that his number one goal, above all, was to "unlock the bondmen's chains and carry free education into every poor man's hut..."[3] After all, it was Stevens in the Pennsylvania State Legislature who was responsible for the start of public schools in the Northeast.[4] Above all, his commitment to Negro suffrage continued to be a common theme until his death on August 11, 1868.

In the summer of 1868, the Radical Republicans' plea to impeach President Andrew Johnson for what they claimed was "high crimes and misdemeanors" over his removal of Secretary of War Edwin Stanton (and mostly because he "repeatedly refused to obey the plain mandate of the party which elected him") gave Stevens one final chance to speak on the House floor.[5] Stevens stood up in Congress and elicited one of his most passionate and longest speeches of his career regarding the direction of government. At the very end of the long speech, Stevens turned to Schuyler Colfax, the Speaker of the House and current Vice-Presidential Nominee of Ulysses S. Grant, and declared:

> My sands are nearly run, and I can only see with
> the eye of faith. I am fast descending the downhill

of life, at the foot of which stands an open grave. But you, sir, are promised length of days and a brilliant career. If you and your compeers can fling away ambition and realize that every human being, however lowly-born or degraded, by fortune is your equal, that every inalienable right which belongs to you belongs also to him, truth and righteousness will spread over the land....[6]

Historian Milton Meltzer wrote that even though Stevens knew he was dying, "feeble as he was, he did not stop working."[7] W.E.B. DuBois agreed that Stevens, "in his last breath...stood true to his principles" and although he was near death, "to the very end he fought on."[8] In addition, the *New York Times* added in an obituary of his life that "his mind did not cease to work" despite his inevitable passing.[9] For example, on July 16, 1868, in which would be his penultimate speech to Congress, Stevens again professed his public feelings on voting rights; Stevens asserted, "I desire that not only freedom but universal suffrage shall be declared a part of the birthright of humanity, a part of the inalienable rights of man, so that....every man who has a soul in his body may be recognized as entitled to the inalienable right of "life, liberty, and the pursuit of happiness..."[10]

On August 11, 1868, Stevens passed away peacefully in bed. Two days later, he was transferred to his home in Lancaster, Pennsylvania, the site of where he established his second law practice in 1842 and lived away from Washington, D.C. Just hours before he died, two black ministers came to his bedside and told him that, "you have the prayers of all the colored people in the country."[11] Not only was Stevens an icon of civil rights to African Americans, but his death was mourned heavily throughout the entire northern half of the nation. Word of his demise "spread like wildfire" as large crowds from all over came to see him laid out.[12] While the curr-

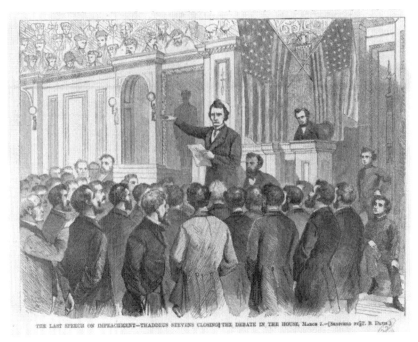

THE LAST SPEECH ON IMPEACHMENT—THADDEUS STEVENS CLOSING THE DEBATE IN THE HOUSE, March 2.—(Sketched by T. R. Davis.)

Stevens giving a speech during President Andrew Johnson's impeachment on March 2, 1868 (Library of Congress)

ent American public may not know who Thaddeus Stevens is, his death was a national time of mourning in 1868—at least in the Northern states. Meltzer explained that a Washington newspaper reported that "no one but Lincoln had ever had such homage paid to him," as long lines of people—both black and white—paid tribute to Stevens deep into the night.[13] When Stevens' official funeral took place two days later in his Lancaster home, fifteen thousand people were said to have attended his Washington, D.C. procession. The Reverend who gave the address at the funeral declared to the crowd that it took an extraordinary person to "confront his contemporaries, to rise above sectional and party interests, to soar above praise and calumny, and to vindicate the claims of right and justice."[14] In tribute for Stevens' accomplishments, the Republican Party in Lancaster nominated him for Congress on the forthcoming ticket, a "fitting tribute to the memory of our most able and distinguished champion of freedom and justice."[15] Not surprisingly, he was elected posthumously in a landslide victory.

Thaddeus Stevens was a man of dignity, who not only believed in true civil rights and equality, but actively dedicated his life to securing these rights. Even though Stevens is no longer looked upon as a villain in American history, his accomplishments and passionate stand for black equality have been lost in the general public's civil rights narrative. Stevens was not just an advocator of African American rights, but a true believer in the complete equality of man who was very much responsible for one of the most known, influential and still controversial Amendments. Biographer, scholar, and historian Hans Trefousse concluded his biography on Stevens by saying he was "imbued with the conviction of equal rights for all" including Chinese and Indians with blacks. Furthermore, while Stevens claimed his life to be a failure by his own standards of never being able to secure full rights for African Americans, his idealistic perspective on equality was well beyond his years. Stevens worked for an interracial democracy in an era that suggests such a social experiment would have been impossible—therefore, "he assuredly deserves to be remembered."[16]

In a fitting end to his life, Stevens searched hard to find a racially integrated cemetery for his final resting place; he ultimately chose Schreiner's Cemetery in Lancaster where his inscription was a reflection of everything he stood for. His inscription read:

> *I repose in this quiet and secluded spot,*
> *Not from any natural preference for solitude*
> *But, finding any other Cemeteries limited*
> *   as to Race by Charter rules,*
> *I have chose this that I might illustrate*

in my death
The Principles which I advocated
Through a long life:
EQUALITY OF MAN BEFORE HIS
CREATOR

Thaddeus Stevens' choice to be buried under these words and in an integrated cemetery, only three years after the Civil War, remains a fitting summary for a man who in a time of extreme racial prejudice fought for civil rights until his final breath ran out.

Seven months following Stevens' death, former Union General Ulysses S. Grant would be sworn in as president with the responsibility of continuing the Republicans' fight for black civil rights and Stevens' past plea for African American suffrage. Although Grant not did necessarily come into office with civil rights on the forefront of his agenda—reuniting the country was always his top priority—the issue of black rights soon became a pressing concern. Frankly, the issues of emancipation and reunion became intricately tied together. Behind the mandate of the Republican Party and the remaining Radicals in Congress, Grant pushed ahead with Stevens' goal of black suffrage in the subsequent years following his death.

PART II

ULYSSES S. GRANT

Fifteenth Amendment of the
Constitution of the United States of America

Section 1. The right of citizens of the United States to vote shall not be denied or abridged by the United States or by any State on account of race, color, or previous condition of servitude.

Section 2. The Congress shall have power to enforce this article by appropriate legislation.

chapter five
"THE AMERICAN SPHINX"

"He is the concentration of all that is American."

– Union soldier Theodore Lyman, 1864, on General Grant

The 1936 Academy Award-winning film *Mr. Deeds Goes to Town* illustrated all there was to know about the legacy of Ulysses S. Grant. The film's main character, Longfellow Deeds, an idealistic and naïve man from a small town, inherits $200 million dollars and flies to New York City to deal with the legal proceedings. Overtaken by Louise "Babe" Bennett, a selfish and cynical reporter, she asks which site he would most like to see in the entire city—Deeds chooses Ulysses S. Grant's Tomb. When they arrive, Deeds is in awe of the memorial; however, Bennett mistakes Deeds' silence for disappointment and explains that it is common to feel that way toward Grant. Deeds, surprised by her comments, replies in earnest that,

> I see a small Ohio farm boy becoming a great solider. I see thousands of marching men. I see General Lee with a broken heart, surrendering, and I can see the beginning of a new nation, like Abraham Lincoln said. And I can see that Ohio boy being inaugurated as President. Things like that can only happen in a country like America.

Historian Joan Waugh explained that this dialogue "suggested both the lingering impression of Grant, and, in Bennett's sarcastic remarks, his legacy's descent."[1] It is through this framework that the history of U.S. Grant should be understood; Grant was one of the most beloved Americans ever to serve his country, "equal in stature to George Washington and Abraham Lincoln" yet his "legacy disappeared from popular memory with shocking rapidity."[2] Through a mix of intense revision and misunderstanding on U.S. Grant's life, his extraordinary and admirable impact on civil rights has been almost completely hidden from civil rights narratives, at best.[3]

Ulysses S. Grant—Union General during the Civil War and 18th President of the United States—was the unlikeliest of civil rights heroes. In contrast to Thaddeus Stevens, Grant was not a fiery orator nor was he a born-to-be politician; in fact, Grant was a "perfectly ordinary human being."[4] Grant biographer Brooks D. Simpson expanded on this idea that Grant was a normal man "who accomplished extraordinary tasks."[5] Due to his soft-spoken nature and humble personality, Grant's name is rarely connected to any type of civil rights leadership. However, many of the immense black gains during Reconstruction can be linked back to President Grant and in some instances such as the Fifteenth Amendment, can be directly attributed to his actions. While other civil rights leaders campaigned their cause through words, Grant held real power—both as a general and as president—and used his power to the betterment of society. Furthermore, he knew that the "sacred heart" of Reconstruction was to "protect the Negro in his new freedom" and that they would fall back into oppression unless the "strong arm of the Federal government protected him."[6] As the former Union General, Grant was especially invested in making sure the country protected the goals of the bloody Civil War, including protecting the rights of freedmen and women in which the war emancipated. Therefore, his actions in this area deserve to be analyzed with renewed precision.

An All-American Hero

Grant was born in Ohio in 1822 to Jesse Grant and Hannah Simpson, the former having had ancestral roots in America dating back to 1630.[7] By the standards of the time, Grant had a relatively normal boyhood with little note of anything spectacular that would hint at his later fame; he attended a mix of local and boarding schools, and while he was not a stellar student, he was level-headed and independent, both traits that Abraham Lincoln would admire in Grant years later.[8] In addition, Grant had a proclivity for mathematics hat also would

A drawing of Grant's home in St. Louis, 1865 (Library of Congress)

reappear through his adept military skills. Throughout Grant's early years, his father expressed strong antislavery feelings, which may have had an affect on Ulysses at an early age.[9] By 1837, Jesse Grant had pushed young Ulysses for the United States Military Academy. Two years later, Grant was accepted into the class of 1843, passed his admission test, and entered the academy. "A military life had no charms for me," Grant stated in 1839, "and I had not the faintest idea of staying in the army even if I should be graduated, which I did not expect."[10] After four years of both successes and challenges, Grant in fact graduated from West Point in 1843 and was sent to Missouri's Jefferson Barracks in St. Louis County. After his Fourth Infantry was transferred to Louisiana in response to the Mexican-American War, he gained his first taste of war and was quickly promoted.[11] During these years, Grant "transformed from a physically immature boy into a man and a professional solider."[12] In addition, his entrance into war also had a profound effect on his initial dissatisfactions on slavery as his experiences made Grant aware of slavery's belligerent role in shaping the Mexican-American War.[13] Even more, Grant disapprovingly wrote that, "I regard the war as one of the most unjust ever waged by a stronger against a weaker nation."[14] Grant remained in the peacetime army following the Mexican-American War and despite his promotion to Captain, he resigned from the army in 1854.

Grant moved to St. Louis to reunite with his beloved wife Julia and attempted to earn a living as a farmer. However, from 1854-1859, Grant failed in doing so; during these years, Grant struggled financially and lost whatever value his crops had acquired following the Panic of 1857.[15] Yet, despite the extremely tough economic times where Grant even pawned his watch off for money so his family could celebrate Christmas, he displayed a deep sense of morality regarding slavery.[16] "A northerner alone and silenced in a world of slaveowners," neighbors often questioned why Grant did not use his father-in-law Colonel Dent's slaves free of charge when he mightily needed the extra labor and was struggling financially. Despite both of those factors, Grant instead chose to hire free blacks, and "paid them more than the average wage."[17] In 1859, Grant acquired a thirty-five-year-old slave from Colonel Dent and shortly after, went down to the circuit house and emancipated the slave. Historian Jean Edward Smith explained that, "Grant never discussed his motives, but the action speaks for itself. Able-bodied slaves sold for a thousand dollars or more, and Grant surely could have used the money."[18] After Grant failed as a farmer, he moved to Galena, Illinois to work in his father's leather shop. With the Civil War looming, Grant expressed some support for the Republican Party because in 1856 for the first time, there was a "nomination of a Presidential Candidate by a party distinctly opposed to slavery..."[19] Furthermore, "the excruciating division over slavery that tormented America," wrote Grant biographer Geoffrey Perret, "sorely troubled Grant despite all his efforts to avoid confronting it directly."[20] On April 12, 1861, the Civil War had officially commenced, and as the only military veteran in town, Grant eagerly accepted a leadership position.

In Galena, Grant's official entry in the war began as he had been asked to help train the volunteer regi-

A portrait of General Grant during the Civil War (Library of Congress)

ment that responded to Lincoln's call to arms. A month later in May, Grant became the leader of the 21st Illinois Infantry Regiment before eventually rising to Brigadier General. Grant would gain national attention following his modest victory at Belmont, Missouri in 1861 and steadily rose in rank thereafter.[21] From 1861-1863, the Union struggled on the eastern battlefield and suffered on the homefront; however, Grant's spectacular successes at Fort Henry and Fort Donelson provided a bright spot amidst President Lincoln's frustration in the lack of offense by Union generals.[22] With victories at Shiloh (albeit narrowly), Vicksburg, and Chattanooga, by late 1863, "Grant stood as the most successful Union general of the Civil War."[23]

As general, Grant's "unstinting support for emancipation" allowed him to use his powerful position to aid blacks.[24] For example, in 1863 Grant successfully created a refugee camp to aid ex-slaves and "consistently voiced his strong support for African American troops."[25] Following the Emancipation Proclamation that officially put an end to slavery, Grant immediately gave President Lincoln his "hearty support" in having the freedmen join the Union lines and exclaimed that we "have added a powerful ally" and that "they would make good soldiers" in his letter to the President.[26] Not only did Grant demonstrate his positive feelings toward blacks through letters, but he was deeply committed to making sure they had justice as members of the military; in response to reports that African American Union POW's had been abused by Confederate soldiers, General Grant wrote a letter to General Robert E. Lee explaining his commitment to protecting "all persons received into the army of the United States, regardless of color."[27] Overall, emancipation directly impacted the prospects of a Union victory as many African Americans proved to be worthy soldiers. Even more, emancipation gave Grant the opportunity to develop a deep respect towards blacks.

By 1864, President Lincoln had officially placed Grant in charge of the entire Union army and by February, his successes in the Western Theater gave him confidence to devise a plan to defeat the Confederacy in the Eastern Theater of Virginia.[28] Yet, in the spring and summer of 1864, Grant's offensive in Virginia proved costly in terms of bloodshed and more troublesome strategically than expected; however, with the election of 1864 fast approaching and the fall of Atlanta, Georgia by General William Sherman, Lincoln received a huge boost in his efforts for a successful reelection.[29] On the war front, Grant and his Union troops surrounded the Army of Northern Virginia and on April 9, 1865, General Lee surrendered his army to General Grant at Appomattox Court House, Virginia. The end of this bloody war made Grant the supreme hero of the nation; he had defeated the Confederate States of America and helped to permanently end the institution of slavery in the United States. As a result, he dispatched a characteristically modest telegram about the end of the war to Washington, D.C that involved "no brag, no bluster, no stirring words...just a simple statement succinctly summarizing the day's events."[30] Years later during Grant's trip around the world, he admitted that he fought the Civil War "not only to save the Union, but to destroy slavery." When asked if saving the Union was the "dominant sentiment," Grant replied:

> In the beginning, yes...but as soon as slavery fired upon the flag it was felt, we all felt, even those who did not object to slaves, that slavery must be destroyed. We felt that it was a stain to the Union that men should be bought and sold like cattle.[31]

The years following the Civil War from 1865-1868 remained a busy time in Grant's life. As the standing General-in-Chief, Grant was responsible for carrying out the Reconstruction policies that were intended to create military districts in the South and protect the rights of freedmen. Following the 1866 riots in Memphis and New Orleans in which white mobs killed many freedmen, Grant wrote that the unjust violence elicited from him the "same obligation to stand at my post that I did whilst there were rebel armies in the field to contend with."[32] During these years, Grant continued to make sense of how he could use the results of the war to reconcile the Union. Despite his favorable position in President Johnson's administration, Grant "stood with Republicans in making sure that Union victory was…protecting the rights and establishing the citizenship of southern blacks."[33] In 1868, Grant was unanimously nominated by the Republican Party for the presidency. Despite consistently stating that he had no desire to be president, Grant felt an overwhelming sense of responsibility to protect the "results of a costly war"—especially the rights of African Americans.[34] Overall, Grant knew that the war's goals of successfully reuniting the country and emancipating the slaves were still a very fragile proposition as the nation was extremely fractured and the ex-slaves had very little rights. While Grant never had an affinity for politics nor a sense for the public eye, he felt it was his duty to make sure the two goals of the war were solidified in the years following the Civil War.

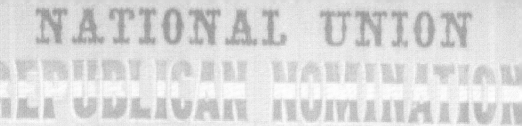

A VISION FOR SUFFRAGE

" The present difficulty, in bringing
all parts of the United States to a
happy unity and love of country
grows out of the prejudice to
color. The prejudice is a senseless
one, but it exists. "

–Ulysses S. Grant, 1866

Due to Congressional Reconstruction and imposed military rule, the election of 1868 was the first election where blacks could vote. In result, Grant was overwhelmingly elected. As president, Grant felt obliged to reunite the country and make sure the nation would avoid such a schism in the future. However, reconciling the goals of the war proved extremely difficult; not only did Grant have the near-impossible duty of bringing together a fractured country, he also became a symbol of liberty for blacks seeking their civil rights. Grant's record on freedmen's rights during his presidency was exemplary as documented through both his rhetoric and more importantly, through his actions. While Grant presided over the Fourteenth Amendment as General-in-Chief and signed the Civil Rights Act of 1875 as president, he also played a pivotal role in making the Fifteenth Amendment—suffrage rights for blacks—become a reality.

In just over a month before he would be sworn in to the Presidency, he spoke at the National Convention of the Colored Men of America on January 20, 1868, summarizing his stance on civil rights:

> I thank the convention of which you are the representatives for the confidence they have expressed, and I hope sincerely that the colored people of the nation may receive every protection which the laws given them. They shall have my efforts to secure such protection. They should prove by their acts, their advancement, prosperity, and obedience to the laws worthy of all privileges the Government has bestowed upon by their future conduct, and prove themselves deserving of all they now claim.[1]

During the first two years of his presidency, Grant's actions paralleled his rhetoric; for example, he had taken a continued interest as president in assuring protection for employees of the Freedman's Bureau.[2] Grant also had appointed an unprecedented number of blacks to federal positions, in which black civil rights advocate George T. Downing thanked President Grant for "giving a rebuke to vulgar prejudices..."[3]

Grant ultimately felt that giving African Americans the right to vote was the most pressing matter for allowing blacks "to shape their own future" and integrate into the Union.[4] Unlike Congressman Thaddeus Stevens and Senator Charles Sumner whose civil rights advocacy had a moralistic undercurrent, Grant's primary goal as president was to unify the fractured country and he felt that granting African Americans the right to vote was extremely important to this Reconstruction goal. However, history suggests that the passage of such an amendment granting black suffrage was far from a foregone conclusion.

Since the end of the Civil War in 1865, passionate antislavery and black rights politicians such as Stevens and Sumner each heavily pushed the issue in their respective chamber. Proposals of suffrage bills—even watered down ones—consistently resulted in stalemates as "it was clear by these defeats that a majority of Republicans were not yet ready for national enfranchisement of Negroes..."[5] In the summer of 1866, the Fourteenth Amendment, which alluded to voting rights but did not fully grant them to blacks, passed both chambers of Congress only because it stripped out the suffrage provision included by Thaddeus Stevens.[6] It was clear that "most congressmen apparently did not intend to risk drowning by swimming against the treacherous current of racial prejudice and opposition to Negro suffrage."[7] Voters in most Northern states decisively rejected black suffrage as Radical Republican Senator Jacob Howard of Michigan admitted that he did not believe any such measure would pass the mandatory ratification process by three-fourths of the states.[8]

When Grant entered office in 1868, he was considered a moderate Republican who was neither a friend nor an ally of Stevens or Sumner; based on his place on the political spectrum, it seemed far-fetched that Grant would align with the Radicals in his party. The rights of freedmen were secondary to his focus on the nation's reunion. In addition, "no

A portrait of Grant as President (Library of Congress)

ground swell of popular support or any great decisive change in public opinion" had occurred in the previous three years.[9] Eventually, Grant realized that his goal of reuniting the country was heavily entwined with emancipation and civil rights, especially suffrage. In addition, Grant also understood that he needed black votes to sustain Republican rule, another reason why he was so heavily invested in securing African American suffrage.

Voting amendments had continued to bounce around in both the House and the Senate since 1867; in 1868 eleven amendments alone were introduced to expand suffrage to blacks, yet, out of all those bills, only one had made it to Committee before failing in a final House vote.[10] While the issue still remained front and center, the prospects of such an amendment grew increasingly dim without a President who could fulfill the Radical Republicans' vision of black suffrage. Therefore, Grant's influence and push as executive of the nation cannot be understated. Historian Frank J. Scaturro agreed that, "Grant played a major role in securing the Fifteenth Amendment..."[11]

Since the Amendment had developed out of Congressional discussions, in what ways, then, did Grant help its passage? When the potential Fifteenth Amendment passed both Congressional chambers in January of 1869, the prospects for ratifying the new Amendment were questionable at best in the months to follow.[12] Knowing that the nation still opposed suffrage, Grant directly addressed the issue in his first inaugural address on March 4, 1869:

> The question of suffrage is one which is likely to agitate the public so long as a portion of the citizens of the nation are excluded from its privileges in any State. It seems to me very desirable that this question should be settled now, and I entertain the hope and express the desire that it may be by the ratification of the fifteenth article of amendment to the Constitution.[13]

Grant needed twenty-eight out of the thirty-seven states to secure ratification, which would prove difficult due to barriers such as moderate Republicans, Democrats, and state legislators who did not want to "commit political suicide" by going against public opinion.[14] Senator William M. Stewart of Nevada—one of the framers of the Fifteenth Amendment—encouraged Grant to use his popularity to help pass black suffrage. Stewart told Grant in 1869 that, "Three-fourths of the States, being the number necessary to adopt the amendment, have already voted for you, and the legislatures of nearly all of them will be in session during the coming winter. The

A commemorative illustration of President Grant signing the Fifteenth
Amendment with other Republican leaders in 1871. Vignettes along the sides
and bottom show African Americans in military service, at school, on the farm,
and voting. (Library of Congress)

number of persons desiring office may not be a majority
of the people, but they are numerous enough to control
the State legislatures so far as complying with any rea-
sonable wish of yours is concerned." Grant, humbled by
Stewart's comment, promised to support the Amendment
at every "proper occasion."[15] In an attempt to heed that
call to action, Grant promptly pushed for ratification and
continued to express "his concern to black Americans"
through letters and correspondence.[16] On top of the Fifteenth Amendment, Grant fought to enforce the
Reconstruction Acts, which provided military protection
for blacks in the South.[17] Due to the large amount of violence including lynchings and assaults against freedmen

specifically, the Reconstruction Act of 1867 created five military districts within the eleven ex-Confederate States (except Tennessee) overlooked by the Federal Government. These military districts attempted to prevent violence and protect the new rights of African Americans.[18]

Grant's determination to secure ratification of the Fifteenth Amendment continued to define his early years as president. His actions—and not necessarily his words—proved critical to the Amendment's survival. In Nebraska, Grant urged the "governor to call a special session to secure ratification there," providing much pressure to Governor Butler.[19] And in Nevada, he "twisted arms" to gain their support in ratifying the Amendment. Most importantly, Grant also influenced Congress to create a mandate that Southern states re-applying for admission into the Union must ratify the Fifteenth Amendment—a key to securing the Amendment's ratification.[20] Grant pleaded for Americans to give freedmen a "fair chance" and let their actions—and not their race—"regulate the treatment and fare" they will receive.[21] On February 3, 1870, the Fifteenth Amendment was ratified in the United States Constitution, forever preventing a citizen's "race, color, or previous condition of solitude" to impact their right to vote in America.

Grant felt that the ratification of the Fifteenth Amendment was a monumental step in securing equal rights for blacks. Following such an accomplishment, Grant took liberty to issue a special commemoration ceremony on March 30, 1870, in front of both chambers of Congress. Deeming that it was "unusual" for both houses to be present, he cited the "vast importance" of the Fifteenth Amendment in which he declared:

> A measure which makes at once four million people voters who were heretofore declared by the highest tribunal in the land not citizens of the

> United States…is indeed a measure of grander importance than any other one act of the kind from the foundation of our free Government to the present day…I repeat that the adoption of the fifteenth amendment to the Constitution creates the greatest civil change and constitutes the most important event that has occurred since the nation came into life.[22]

Furthermore, on April 15, 1870, the *New York Times* reported a gathering of over five thousand people in Washington, D.C., celebrating the ratification of the Amendment. Judge Fisher of the Committee of Arrangements addressed the President and said, "succeeding generations will cherish in their hearts the memory of Washington, Lincoln and Grant as a trio whose memory will be worthy to be commemorated so long as equality and liberty endure with humanity." Grant subtly replied, "I could not say anything to those who are assembled here this evening to convince them any further that I have done of my earnest desire to see the Fifteenth Amendment become a part of the Constitution…I hope those enfranchised by it will prove themselves worthy of its benefits, and to those without it; that all may be mutually benefited by the result."[23] Prominent abolitionist William Lloyd Garrison exclaimed a day earlier at another celebration in Boston that African Americans were eager to "give their hands to President Grant, and let him know that hero, in the Cradle of Liberty, they recognized his course of honor." [24]

Barely a year into his presidency, Grant was able to pave the way for black suffrage and although the Fifteenth Amendment did not end voting discrimination, still, the "passage represented another huge advancement for black Americans, which, like emancipation, had become unimaginable a short while before."[25]

chapter seven
AN UNDESERVING LEGACY

"It seems that one man's destiny in this world is quite as much a mystery as it is likely to be in the next."

–Ulysses S. Grant in his *Personal Memoirs*, 1885

GEN. U.S. GRANT, WRITING HIS MEMOIRS AT MT. MC GREGOR, JUNE 27, 1885 PHOTO BY HOWE? N.Y. © DEC. 2, 1886 – CR. 615654

For the remaining two years of President Grant's first term in office and his subsequent four following his reelection, Grant continued to fight for black rights in a methodical manner. Always feeling the burden of using his executive power to reunite the nation, Grant took upon himself the heavy responsibility of protecting the rights of freedmen, especially voting rights that he had signed, with the utmost sense of urgency. However, protecting black gains was very difficult to do while also attempting to achieve sectional peace; Grant struggled to enact the best policies for African Americans without putting the Republican Party in political jeopardy for he believed that the goals of the Civil War would be lost if the Democrats gained power. Striking a balance between reuniting the country while striving for more black rights was a delicate situation. While not all of his decisions were sound—in fact, some were arguably detrimental to the country—he was always well intentioned. Therefore, he should at least be recognized for his efforts during an unprecedented difficult time in American history.

By 1871, violence against blacks had become a problem as Grant wrote to House Speaker James G. Blaine that the "deplorable state of affairs in some parts of the South" required the "immediate attention of Congress."[1] The Ku Klux Klan had grown all across the country, especially in Southern states, and remained a significant and violent threat not only to freedmen but also to Grant's protective policies. Therefore, Grant signed into law the Enforcement Acts in 1870 and 1871 that were designed to give the Federal Government more power to protect black Americans from Southern violence. The Ku Klux Klan Act of April 1871 also gave an unprecedented amount of power to the Federal Government, providing the government the ability to prosecute individuals through federal attorneys and even allow for military intervention.[2] Yet, feeling that Reconstruction

President Grant signing the Ku Klux Klan Bill in the President's room with Secretary Robeson and General Porter, at the Capitol, April 20, 1871 (Library of Congress)

---

was unfinished in 1872, Grant decided to run for a second term as president and was considered even more so than ever, an advocate in fighting for equality under the law.

Gerrit Smith, a former abolitionist and prominent civil rights advocate wrote that in the face of reelection, Grant "has proved himself to be free from the accursed spirit of caste, and true to the equal rights of men—of the red man and black man as well as the white man."[3] Following Grant's victory in the election of 1872, the former general re-stated his desire to fight for civil rights in his Second Inaugural Address; he declared that:

> The effect of the late civil strife has been to free the slave and make him a citizen. Yet he is not

possessed of the civil rights which citizenship should carry with it. This is wrong and should be corrected. To this correction I stand committed so far as executive influence can avail.[4]

Throughout his second presidential term, Grant's popularity steadily grew within the black population in both the North and the South. For example, Grant received an invitation to attend an African American meeting on civil rights in May of 1872; regretfully, Grant could not attend but wrote that, "I beg to assure however that I sympathize most cordially in any effort to secure for all our people whatever race, nativity or color exercise of those rights to which every Citizen should be entitled."[5] In late November, President Grant spoke to a group of blacks, explaining that he wished "every man in the United States would stand in all respects alike. It must come."[6] Grant was an icon of freedom for African Americans and despite his shortcomings of fully protecting them from the violence and prejudice that permeated the South, his efforts were still clearly recognized by them.

Grant's disappointing remaining years in the White House was filled with various charges of corruption. For example, the Panic of 1873 combined with scandals such as the "Whisky Ring" and Crédit Mobilier Scandal were all negative events that occurred during his second term.[7] In addition, ongoing violence against African Americans in the South forced Grant to continue constant military intervention in Southern states. However, while Grant and the Federal Government "ended the Reconstruction career of the Ku Klux Klan" by destroying the organization, ultimately, he was regrettably unable to stop the violence that plagued elections.[8]

The lone bright spot of his final four years in office was the Civil Rights Act of 1875 that he signed into law. While Grant received many letters from African Americans thanking him for his "loyalty" to them and that the

Civil Rights Act was a "lasting blessing," he also received a barrage of letters urging him to veto it due to the political atmosphere at the time. Even more, Grant received death threats claiming that if he signed the Act, "he would not live one month longer" and another, threatening that he, "shall not live long to enjoy the negro privilege you give him."[9] Yet, despite the hostile environment, Grant declared that the country needed to labor for the guarantee of "equal right and privileges to all men irrespective of nationality, color or religion."[10]

While Grant's reconstruction policies were far from perfect, still, he was firmly dedicated to securing equal rights and did undoubtedly do so in many, many ways. "I have acted in every instance from a conscientious desire to do what was right," Grant wrote in his final address, "Failures have been errors of judgment, not of intent."[11] To address these failures, the vitriolic political landscape and time period, again, must be placed in appropriate context; it was beyond Grant's control that advocating for civil rights was an extremely politically unpopular move that could help push Republicans out of power and tear the nation further apart. Historian and Grant biographer Brooks D. Simpson argued that not only did Grant stop the "threat of a second civil war,'" but acted "skillfully" in enacting his policies, "blending a commitment to principle with due to attention to Republican interests."[12] Grant understood that if Republicans lost power, black Americans' civil rights gains would be in jeopardy yet fighting for civil rights weakened the Republican Party. Despite his overall failures to secure ever-lasting protection of African Americans and complete economic uplift, his passage of the Fifteenth Amendment cannot be overlooked. Suffrage for African Americans had been at the forefront of the civil rights struggle when Grant finally secured suffrage, which also put Republicans in a more favorable position with the acquirement of black votes.

Funeral of Ulysses S. Grant in New York City, 1886 (Library of Congress)

Historian William Gillette wrote that in reference to the Fifteenth Amendment and the fight for black suffrage that it is, "appropriate to rediscover a crucial phase of national Reconstruction."[13] Though flawed, the Fifteenth Amendment was a gigantic landmark for African Americans.

Grant spent the remaining years of his life in relative peace; immediately after he left the White House, Grant and his wife Julia dedicated two years to traveling the world and upon their return, moved to New York. Yet in 1883, Grant was diagnosed with incurable throat cancer. In the three years prior to his death, Grant wrote his famous *Personal Memoirs of U.S. Grant* through an incredible amount of pain from the throat cancer. Just as he had shown throughout his life, the courage to complete such a project was historic in itself.[14] On the morning of July 23, 1885, Ulysses S. Grant passed away, as the great general and former president's death made the country mourn in ways it never had before.

The nation's response to Grant's death is hard to realistically quantify over one hundred and thirty years later; this is due to the fact that Grant was not only the most popular man in America, but was also a symbol of unity that no person would ever again embody. Over a million and half alone were said to have gathered at his funeral on August 8, 1885, in addition to the thousands of smaller memorial ceremonies that took place through-out the country.[15] The Chicago City Council exclaimed that the "death of Gen. Grant is a calamity affecting the entire Nation" and a newspaper in South Carolina wrote that his death, "will be honestly felt as a national affliction all over the wide Union, without reference to section or party."[16] For a still bitterly fractured nation, Grant's death—unlike other prominent statesman such as Thaddeus Stevens—brought together both the North *and* the South in mourning. The amount of praise that show-ered Grant remained endless; the Mayor of New York explained that, "there is no man for whom, as an Ameri-can, I have a higher respect than for Gen. Grant."[17] Frankly, another eulogy phrase stated that, "no words can quicken the impression this man has made upon his Nation and his generation," summarizing Grant's "larger-than-life" legacy following his death."[18]

Ulysses S. Grant was ranked in the same echelon as George Washington and Abraham Lincoln at the end of the twentieth century. One could argue that Grant was the most famous American—living or dead. Yet, why have those men reached legendary status while Grant's name toils in mediocrity? For a man who grew from such humble origins, was responsible for saving the Union, and attempted to unify the country in arguably the most difficult time in American history, this question remains

mind-boggling. There are a variety of reasons that an-
swer this question, most notably that the "Lost Cause"
version of Grant as a drunk, bloodthirsty general and
corrupt, dictatorial president permeated the history books
in the first half of the twentienth century. Fortunately, recent scholarship has proved these perspectives
inaccurate as Grant's legacy continues to climb—
although it will most likely never reach its almost-mythic
level it had following his death. In addition, historians
have constantly criticized Grant for his inconsistent policy, yet, none have been "able to suggest how he could
have forged a policy that would have achieved both sectional reconciliation and justice for black Americans."
Alluding to the impossibility of such a task, "perhaps it
was not his failure after all."[19]

Hidden within modern scholarship is Grant's remarkable record on civil rights; while his life will always
be controversial, his stance on the rights of African
Americans remains well documented. However, Grant's
name, one could argue, is rarely—if ever—connected
with such a cause. "Grant's messages condemning racial
violence and defending political equality regardless of
color," argued historian Frank Scaturro, "remain a singu-
lar presidential demonstration of eloquence in the realm
of civil rights in the nineteenth century."[20] While it is true
that Grant probably did not think of himself as a civil
rights leader—in fact he would never use such a term—
the truth remains that his actions justify him to be one.

Although the debate on whether Grant was actually successful in gaining and protecting the rights of
freedpeople during Reconstruction may never be settled,
his actions as both a general and president undoubtedly
increased the civil rights of African Americans. The Fifteenth Amendment and the Civil Rights Act of 1875 both
were passed under his watch as he actively legislated to
"maintain political equality and rights therein, irrespective

A picture of Grant's Tomb in New York City, taken in 1899 (Library of Congress)

of race and color."[21] Though his oratory did not match future civil rights leaders, he constantly worried "about the great unresolved issue of the Civil War and Reconstruction—the place of blacks in American life."[22] In an Associated Press interview with U.S. Senator Blanche K. Bruce of Mississippi in 1878, Bruce stated that Grant's name was one of the most cherished names to African Americans in the South. Bruce continued that:

> ...among the most satisfactory interviews I had with Gen. Grant at Paris was one in which he declared that he had no apprehensions relative to the success of colored people as citizens of the United States. He cited notable instances of success...He affirmed that observation of the colored people...convinced him that their emancipation

and enfranchisement was not a mistake, but a wise and beneficent measure, which the future history of the race would vindicate.[23]

While Grant's overall actions have indeed been vindicated, one can hope that his civil rights legacy will some day get vindicated, too.

PART III

CHARLES SUMNER

Civil Rights Act of 1875

Whereas it is essential to just government we recognize the equality of all men before the law, and hold that it is the duty of government in its dealings with the people to mete out equal and exact justice to all, of whatever nativity, race, color, or persuasion, religious or political; and it being the appropriate object of legislation to enact great fundamental principles into law: Therefore,

Be it enacted, That all persons within the jurisdiction of the United States shall be entitled to the full and equal enjoyment of the accommodations, advantages, facilities, and privileges of inns, public conveyances on land or water, theaters, and other places of public amusement; subject only to the conditions and limitations established by law, and applicable alike to citizens of every race and color, regardless of any previous condition of servitude.

SEC. 2. That any person who shall violate the foregoing section by denying to any citizen, except for reasons by law applicable to citizens of every race and color, and regardless of any previous condition of servitude, the full enjoyment of any of the accommodations, advantages, facilities, or privileges in said section enumerated, or by aiding or inciting such denial, shall, for every such offense, forfeit and pay the sum of five hundred dollars to the person aggrieved thereby, . . . and shall also, for every such offense, be deemed guilty of a misdemeanor, and, upon conviction thereof, shall be fined not less than five hundred nor more than one thousand dollars, or shall be imprisoned not less than thirty days nor more than one year . . .

SEC. 3. That the district and circuit courts of the United States shall have exclusively of the courts of the several States, cognizance of all crimes and offenses against, and violations of, the provisions of this act. . .

SEC. 4. That no citizen possessing all other qualifications which are or may be prescribed by law shall be disqualified for service as grand or petit juror in any court of the United States, or of any State, on account of race, color, or previous condition of servitude; and any officer or other person charged with any duty in the selection or summoning of jurors who shall exclude or fail to summon any citizen for the cause aforesaid shall, on conviction thereof, be deemed guilty of a misdemeanor, and be fined not more than five thousand dollars.

SEC. 5. That all cases arising under the provisions of this act ... shall be renewable by the Supreme Court of the United States, without regard to the sum in controversy ...

chapter eight
A REBEL FROM THE START

" Man, as an individual, is capable of
indefinite improvement, so long as
he lives."
– Charles Sumner, 1842

Charles Sumner's most recent biographer, historian David Donald, defined Sumner as "a man inflexibly committed to a set of basic ideas as moral principles."[1] Those principles that defined Charles Sumner were grounded in equality, social justice, and civil rights. Yet, Donald contended that Charles Sumner's history was "unique" because rarely, if ever, has a man with these distinguished principles garnered such incredible political power in the history of the United States.[2]

Sumner lived his life as a means to fight for black equality, his source of passion as a U.S. Senator. While the national conversation on black rights had begun to taper following the passage of the Fifteenth Amendment in 1870, Charles Sumner fought to keep the issue alive recognizing that blacks were still far from equal. Sumner had enormous influence on the passage of the Fourteenth Amendment and earlier Civil Rights Acts, yet, it was a lifelong struggle for granting freedmen complete social rights—an unprecedented belief that would not truly come to fruition until the 1960s—that sets him apart as one of the pre-eminent civil rights leaders in history. Yet, his aggressive, polarizing demeanor in the Senate Chamber and the fact that his 1875 Civil Rights Act eventually was ruled unconstitutional eight years later both seem to have diminished his place in civil rights history. Regardless, Charles Sumner deserves to be recognized for being the "prophet and champion" of black equality during an era when few stood up to the prejudice and hatred with the zeal, passion, and most importantly, action that he did.[3] Therefore, it is important to explain the context of how Sumner developed such a passion for reform. While historian Beverly Wilson Palmer argued that there was little evidence during his adolescence that he would become an anti-slavery leader, there were still a number of experiences in Sumner's early life that shaped his curiosity on U.S. slavery.[4]

The Origins

Charles Sumner was born in 1811 to a modest family in Boston. Yet, unlike Thaddeus Stevens, there is "revealingly reticent" amount of information about his boyhood.[5] Sumner had a distant relationship with his father, spending his adolescence trying to win his father's approval. In that framework, Sumner enrolled at Harvard University where he generally excelled not necessarily in the self-described "dull curriculum" but "for the love of study and cultivating his mind."[6] His interest in public speaking would foreshadow his oratorical legacy in the U.S. Senate; for example, one of his college classmates contended that he was "one of the best declaimers in the class" as he spoke in school with "the same type of subdued eloquence" that he would use for "real and important actions in his public life" in the future.[7]

Shortly after Sumner graduated from Harvard in 1830, he entered Harvard Law School and passed the Bar Exam in 1834. He then went on to teach at Harvard for the subsequent three years. However, in 1834, Sumner saw slaves in the South for the first time, declaring, "I have now an idea of ye blight upon that part of our country in which they live."[8] It was following this exposure that "Sumner began to study the issue of slavery more intently."[9] Sumner's intellectual background and knowledge of law led him to think deeply about the moral quandary of slavery as he immersed himself in antislavery texts including William Lloyd Garrison's *The Liberator*.[10] Despite being upset with its harsh tone, Sumner exclaimed years later that, "It was the first paper I ever subscribed for. I did it in the sincerity of my early opposition."[11] Upon growing dissatisfaction with law, Sumner traveled to Europe for almost three years, returning in 1840. From 1840-1845, Sumner slowly began to abandon his law practice while "his popularity grew as a consequence of his antislavery writings."[12] One of those writings disagreed with the well-known Whig, Daniel Webster—former senator, congressman, and three-term Secretary of State who had been one of the most prominent politicians of the Antebellum Period.

However, the Fourth of July of 1845 was a turning point in Sumner's life that would emphatically propel him into the public eye; Sumner was chosen by the Mayor of Boston to give the prestigious and historic annual Fourth of July Oration in front of the whole city, including the military.[13] While Sumner informed the Mayor and City Council that his topic would be on International Peace, he

A sign entitled "Pioneers of Freedom," made up of former abolitionists in 1866, with Charles Sumner at the top (Library of Congress)

instead shocked everyone in attendance by utterly attacking warfare on every level:

> *The True Grandeur of Humanity is in moral elevation, sustained, enlightened, and decorated by the intellect of man...But War crushes, with bloody heel, all beneficence, all happiness, all justice, all that is God-like in man. It suspends every commandment of the Decagogue. It sets at*

naught every principle of the Gospel. It silences all law, human as well as divine, except only the blasphemous code of its own, the *Laws of War.*[14]

Historian Kirt H. Wilson argued that this speech—although not directly about slavery or civil rights—led to a number of important consequences for Sumner. While it undoubtedly created enemies and generated hostile responses from friends, politically, it pushed Sumner past moderates in either party and sparked his popularity among a "growing group of social activists."[15] In addition, Sumner became a local leader in Boston over the nationwide controversy swirling around whether Texas—which had just been admitted into the Union in 1845—should become a free state or slave state.[16] In 1848, Charles Sumner helped create the Free Soil Party, an anti-slavery party focused on the opposition of extending slavery, and a year later, Sumner argued on behalf of a black father fighting against school segregation.[17] In *Roberts v. City of Boston,* Sumner defended Sarah Roberts, a 5-year old African American girl, whose father Benjamin Roberts attempted to enroll in a white school. In this Supreme Court case, Sumner argued that segregating schools defined what it meant to be unequal. Sumner declared:

> In the exercise of these powers they cannot put colored children to personal inconvenience greater than that of white children. Still further, they cannot brand a whole race with the stigma of inferiority and degradation, constituting them into a Caste. They cannot in any way violate that fundamental right of all citizens, *Equality before the law.*[18]

Yet, Sumner lost the case and unfortunately knew that this ruling would set the precedent for the "separate but equal" doctrine later established by the 1896 *Plessy v. Ferguson* landmark decision. By 1849, Sumner had already grasped the "principles that have been validated by modern sociology" as it took over a century later in 1954's *Brown v. Board of Education* Supreme Court decision to realize Sumner's vision for full integration.[19]

Following Charles Sumner's successful election to the U.S. Senate from Massachusetts in 1851 as a Free Soil Party candidate, he immediately began his campaign against slavery. In his first major speech entitled "Freedom National, Slavery Sectional," Sumner attacked slavery as an institution and singled out the Fugitive Slave Act for its unconstitutionality.[20] Following Sumner's three and half hour oration, Senator Salmon P. Chase of Ohio exclaimed that his colleague's speech would mark "an era in American history."[21] Furthermore, Sumner's speech elevated his status in the Senate as one of the foremost leaders of civil rights. Politically, Sumner was uncommitted to joining any political party for his focus was on the anti-slavery issue and little else; it was not until 1855 that Sumner officially began to align with the Republican Party.

On May 19, 1856, in one of the most famous—or infamous—events in Senate history, the Massachusetts Senator gave a similar speech condemning slavery, dubbed "The Crime again Kansas." During a two-day tirade that directly attacked Southern Senators and the popular sovereignty doctrine in reference to Kansas, Sumner declared that, "Not in any common lust for power did this uncommon tragedy have its origin. It is the rape of a virgin Territory, compelling it to the hateful embrace of Slavery; and it may be clearly traced to a depraved longing for a new slave State, the hideous offspring of such a crime...."[22] The doctrine of popular sovereignty attempted to have each newly-admitted territory vote on whether they would become a slave or free territory—a premise that Sumner obviously thought was beyond abominable. On May 22, two days after the beginning of the speech, Senator Preston Brooks of South Carolina—the cousin of South Carolina Senator Andrew Butler whom Sumner viciously criticized—approached Sumner at his desk and after exchanging a few words, attacked him with his cane, striking him fifteen to twenty times until Sumner could finally break away. However, his head was "bruised and gashed, and the flow of blood so copious as to drench his clothes... as he eventually fell unconscious on the Senate floor."[23] Following the attack, Sumner became a martyr for the anti-slavery cause as "hundreds wrote of their sympathy" in letters to him.[24]

A portrait of Sumner in 1859 (Library of Congress)

The physical and psychological damage from the attack prevented Sumner from returning to the U.S. Senate for almost three years. Upon his return in late 1859 at the eve of the Civil War, Sumner's fervor against slavery remained in tact; he spoke in 1861 that, "It is often said that war will make an end of slavery. This is probable; but it is surer still that the overthrow of slavery will make an end of the war.... A simple declaration that all men within the lines of the United States troops are freemen will be in strict conformity with the Constitution and also with the precedent. The Constitution knows no man as slave..."[25]

At the outset of the Civil War in 1861, Sumner immediately approached President Abraham Lincoln and "pledged his support, heart and soul" to urge him to use his wartime powers to emancipate the slaves.[26] Throughout the course of the Civil War, Sumner continued to heavily push Lincoln toward emancipation, enjoying good relations with the President despite their differences.[27] While Sumner was already known as a leading abolitionist who "did all he could to build up anti-slavery sentiment in Congress," his efforts during the war increased to almost obsessive tactics; he even used the death of a senator as an excuse to speak on the issue of slavery.[28] Historian and Sumner biographer David Donald wrote that during the wartime years, "so vigorously and so frequently did Sumner speak on the slavery issue" that many colleagues openly sneered about Sumner's proclivity for African Americans. Furthermore, while most historians agreed that the cause of the Civil War was complex, Sumner had "no difficulty accepting a war that would simply put an end to slavery."[29]

However, by 1862, Sumner began to grow frustrated with Lincoln's lack of commitment to declaring emancipation, criticizing the President and hurting his own chances of reelection. Although Sumner was eventually able to gain reelection, he felt it was his duty to continue impelling the President to issue the final emancipation edict despite other Republican losses in the election.[30] The Massachusetts Senator continued to advise Lincoln in both domestic and foreign issues with varying success, often times creating enemies within his own party because of his self-centered and compulsive views on emancipation. Still, Sumner was an important voice in the Senate during the Civil War, constantly advocating to free the slaves and for a repeal of the Fugitive Slave Law. When the aforementioned law was finally repealed on June 23, 1864, Sumner stated how happy he was as the repeal "closes one chapter of my life. I was chosen to the Senate in order to do this work."[31] With the reconstruction of a shattered nation about to begin, Sumner's passion that had grown at Harvard as a young man would reach its pinnacle during his final nine years in the Senate.

chapter nine
THE "CROWNING WORK" OF RECONSTRUCTION

"Show me a creature, with lifted countenance looking to heaven, made in the image of God, and I show you a MAN, who, of whatever country or race, whether browned by equatorial sun or blanched by northern cold, is with you a child of the Heavenly Father, and equal with you in all the rights of Human Nature. You cannot deny these rights without impiety...you cannot deny these rights without peril to the Republic...By the same title that we claim Liberty do we claim Equality also. One cannot be denied without the other. What is Equality without Liberty? What is Liberty without Equality? One is the complement of the other. The two are necessary to begin and complete the circle of American citizenship. They are inseparable organs through which the people have their national life."
– Charles Sumner, "Equality of Man," 1866

Just as one door had closed in Sumner's life with the complete abolition of slavery, another had opened; due to a Union victory in the Civil War and 4 million ex-slaves freed, Sumner shifted his focus to civil rights and various Reconstruction proposals. Sumner—a Republican since the mid-1850s—joined with other Radical members of his party to oppose the new President Andrew Johnson. From 1865-1870, Sumner continued to fight towards securing black rights; specifically, he isolated himself in the Chamber for not willing to compromise on a variety of issues, especially the Fourteenth Amendment, for he had chosen "the high road of morality while his colleagues had fallen into the slough of compromise with slavery."[1] However, despite his stubborn opposition to the Fourteenth Amendment so he could propose his own supplementary bills to grant greater rights to blacks, Sumner eventually voted for its passage.[2] During the later years of the decade, Sumner continued to be a polarizing figure in the Senate, fighting for black rights that seemed, at the time, overly idealistic; for example, his feelings on full integration in public schools and full social equality (which will be discussed later in the chapter). These ideas and his vision of equality would not be recognized until the 1960s Civil Rights Movement. Yet, following the passage of the Fifteenth Amendment, Charles Sumner "renewed his endeavor to win more precise legislation" for African Americans and went to the extremes to make his dream a reality with the Civil Rights Bill of 1875.[3]

However, since African Americans had now added suffrage to their list of basic rights, the problem of black equality had generally thought to have been solved. Yet, Sumner passionately felt that another civil rights bill was absolutely necessary to securing equal rights to all citizens in America. Attached to an amnesty bill in May of 1870, Sumner's bill would declare complete equal rights to blacks. Sumner read out loud to the Senate chamber that this bill would provide:

> ...that all citizens of the United States, without the distinction of race, color, previous condition of servitude, are entitled to the equal and impartial enjoyment of any accommodation, advantage or privilege...every law, statute, ordinance, regulation, or custom, whether national or State...making any discriminations against any person on account of color, by the use of the word 'white' would be repealed.[4]

While the Fourteenth Amendment granted African Americans basic rights, Sumner's bill offered African Americans unprecedented social rights and immunity to discrimination in the public sphere. In essence, his bill guaranteed equal access to public accommodations such as churches, cemeteries, jury duty, and most importantly, public schools.[5] This bill would be Sumner's lasting legacy and though he failed to see it pass before he died in 1874, it "represented the fullest, and final, formulation of his equal-rights doctrine..."[6]

Securing basic black suffrage in an extremely prejudiced country and still politically hostile environment had already proved to be an incredibly hard measure for President Grant. Yet, for Sumner to try and pass another civil rights bill that granted full citizenship and social equality to African Americans—only seven years since emancipation nonetheless—was almost ludicrous; his bill tried to create the type of harmonious union that would only be enforced almost a century later by the 1964 Civil Rights Act. Historian Eric Foner argued that Sumner, "repudiated the legitimacy of separate but equal facilities and that equivalent differed from equality" and challenged the nation to "live up to" its principles of equal rights.[7] Predictably, Sumner's bill failed to move out of Committee in both 1870 and in 1871 despite his best eff-

THE RADICAL PARTY ON A HEAVY GRADE.

An 1868 election cartoon predicting the victory of Democrat Horatio Seymour in the presidential race. Seymour's head hovers above the White House, complacently watching a group of struggling Republicans. On the right side, Sumner explains, "Why! Old Thad has fallen off the platform!" in reference to Thaddeus Stevens (Library of Congress)

orts to move it forward. However, in a formal attempt to arouse support for his civil rights proposal, Sumner delivered a powerful speech to the Senate on January 15, 1872, which echoed the rhetoric of the landmark *Brown v. Board of Education* decision over eighty years later; Sumner declared that slavery was still present in the country and explained that while some members thought slavery was dead, they were wrong.[8] "Again the barbarous tyranny stalks into this Chamber, denying to a whole race the equal rights promised by a just citizenship," Sumner vehemently explained, "If not in body, at least in spirit or as a ghost making our country hideous, the ancient criminal [of slavery] yet lingers among us, insisting upon the continued degradation of a race."[9]

Charles Sumner's epic speech on the Senate floor

could only be compared to Thaddeus Stevens' fiery rhetoric five years earlier in the House; even more so than Stevens, Sumner attacked the hypocritical principles of the United States with the rhetoric reminiscent of a later era. Sumner continued to give examples of prominent African American leaders such as Frederick Douglass who had been oppressed and had "suffered from a plain denial of equal rights." "Who that has a heart can listen to the story without indignation and shame?" asked Sumner, "who can with a spark of justice to illumine his soul can hesitate to denounce the wrong?"[10] In his rousing speech, Sumner touted that the United States was a republic in name only and that in reality was only a "soulless mockery." On his attack on the Declaration of Independence, Sumner insisted that,

> ...it is no axiom to announce grandly that all white men are equal in rights, nor is it an axiom to announce with grandeur that all equal in rights, but coloured persons have no rights except to testify. Nor is it a self-evident truth, as declared, for no truth is self-evident which is not universal. The asserted limitation destroys the original Declaration, making it a ridiculous sham...[11]

Despite the speech, his Civil Rights Act still could not find enough prolonged traction to gain the two-thirds majority it needed to pass in the Senate. Finally, in May of 1872, Sumner again attached his bill to another amnesty provision that was expected to pass; unfortunately, Sumner's proposal was again defeated in a vote for a third time. Edward L. Pierce wrote in the Massachusetts Senator's memoir that, "It will be hard to find in our history parallels to such pertinacity as Sumner's repeated efforts to carry his civil-rights bill at this session."[12]

Although Charles Sumner's bill was constantly being struck down in committees between 1872 and 1874, his passion and desire to grant complete equal rights to

African Americans remained his sole focus. During those years, Sumner received and wrote numerous letters from and to blacks, championing their cause. For example, in a letter he wrote to the Committee of Arrangements for the Celebration of the Anniversary of the Emancipation on April 16, 1873, Sumner promised to work to continue securing black rights and declared, "until your equality in civil rights is assured, the pillar of your citizenship is like the column of honor of Washington, -- unfinished and imperfect."[13]

A drawing of Charles Sumner holding his Civil Rights Bill (Library of Congress)

In response to another letter from the chairman of an African American citizens meeting about public schooling, Sumner responded on June 22, 1873, that there "shall be no distinction of color" in regards to education and "to call it in question is simply ridiculous." Furthermore, Sumner wrote that the duty of the Legislature was to make sure all schools are open to everyone and that "the time has come for those who love justice to speak out...too long have colored fellow-citizens been deprived of their rights..."[14]

On the first day of the 43rd Session of Congress on

January 27, 1874, Sumner gave one more impassioned plea to get his Civil Rights Bill out of the Judiciary Committee; he explained that during the past four years his bill had been voted on with little consideration and always at the end of sessions. Sumner declared at the end of his speech that this bill must no longer sit in Committee and that "the bill is an urgent necessity" that "is manifest everyday in the outrages to which the colored race are exposed, not only in travel and at hotels, but still more in the children of their homes, who are shut out from those schools where they ought to receive practicality, as well as by lesson, the great duty of Equality."[15] With Sumner's health faltering, the Massachusetts Senator passed away unexpectedly a few months later on March 11, 1874. Just hours before his death, Sumner told New Jersey Senator Frederick Frelinghuysen, "You must take care of my civil rights bill—my bill, the civil rights bill, don't let it fail." An hour later, Frederick Douglass also visited Sumner before he died, in which Sumner also exclaimed, "Don't let the bill fail."[16]

Barely a month after Sumner's death, the Judiciary Committee that had shunned the bill for the past two years, felt favorably on the bill possibly "in respect to Sumner's memory."[17] Historian Bertram Wyatt-Brown also suggested that "there is good reason to believe that the Senate momentarily succumbed to a contrite sentimentalism" regarding Charles Sumner's death.[18] Even more, historian Eric Foner argued that the reason the bill had survived at all "was due to the tireless advocacy of Charles Sumner."[19] Controversial debate between Republicans and Democrats ensued in the Senate as many Republicans would not let the Senate adjourn without the passage of the bill.[20] In June of 1874, the Senate indeed passed Sumner's bill, which was then sent to the House of Representatives. After vigorous debate and compromises in the House, they removed the school desegregation clause and passed an edited version of Sumner's bill in January 1875. Two months later, the Senate passed the House version of the Civil Rights Bill and President Grant signed it into law on March 1, 1875.[21] Though the bill lacked the school desegregation clause that Sumner passionately fought for, the perseverance and tenacity of Charles Sumner in his fight for African American rights had been honored with the passage of his beloved—and unprecedented—Civil Rights Act of 1875.

Yet, assessing the 1875 Act remains a controversial measure without a clear consensus of opinion; many historians feel that the omission of a school desegregation clause, the lack of enforcement, and the Supreme Court decision in 1883 claiming it was unconstitutional made the Act "a little more than an anomaly in the history of race relations in the nineteenth century."[22] For example, Foner wrote that few blacks actually challenged the discriminatory acts against them in court and years prior to 1883, the "law had become a dead letter."[23] However, other historians, such as Kirt H. Wilson, argued that this Act held extreme importance. While Wilson understood that "its immediate effects were minimal," it did effectively hold a "powerful symbolic presence within the African American community."[24] Similar to both the Reconstruction Amendments, the Civil Rights Act of 1875 also holds importance in the present day and especially to the Civil Rights Movement of the 1960s. The famous Civil Rights Act of 1964, which officially granted social equality in the public sphere to African Americans, specifically copied many provisions of the 1875 Act. Regardless, Sumner's Civil Rights Act of 1875 was "a milestone in the evolution of America's civil rights history" and should be recognized as such.[25]

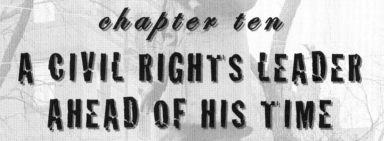

chapter ten
A CIVIL RIGHTS LEADER AHEAD OF HIS TIME

"Whatever he may have been, he is now the same as ourselves. Our rights are his rights; our equality his equality; our privilege and immunities are his possession."
– Charles Sumner, 1842

Close friend, secretary, and biographer of Charles Sumner, Moorfield Storey, wrote that Sumner was, "no politician in the ordinary sense. He saw clearly what was right, and he devoted his life with absolute singleness of purpose and unwavering courage to the pursuit of the ends which his conscience approved....His gaze was fixed on a distant goal, and he did not stop to look at what lay in the path."[1] That distant goal that Storey referred to was Sumner's vision for a world where all men actually were created equal and where peace reigned supreme. Sumner was focused on these principles to a fault, isolating himself from others on racial issues that he knew were inhumane but that the United States would not fully address until over a full century later. Yet, despite his political shortcomings, Sumner should be—and was following his death—remembered with such passion that it remains unfathomable that his name in popular culture rarely brings up a similar notation.

Charles Sumner passed away on March 11, 1874, a day after collapsing on the Senate floor. In the days and weeks that followed, Sumner's death caused a nationwide stir, especially in the Senate itself; a resolution passed two days after his death by the Joint Special Committee created measures for senators and congressmen to speak about the life of Charles Sumner which would be gathered in a Memorial Volume with other eulogies and orations on Sumner. This Volume was printed in the thousands for use in both State and National Legislatures, for every city and town in Massachusetts, and to be given to various state officials.[2] While numerous influential Civil War Era senators and congressmen—including Thaddeus Stevens—had died before him, none had a large posthumous commemorative volume, published by the Legislature, such as the one that Sumner did. The day after Sumner died, Massachusetts Governor W.B. Mashburn spoke on behalf of the State:

> For years one of the most prominent and influential citizens of the United States, he was recognized by the civilized world as one of the foremost advocates of struggling humanity. Thus acknowledged at home and abroad, his death will be deeply mourned...by every people and country reaching out for a higher and free life....His moral integrity stands out as a sublime figure....While the atmosphere around him was foul with corruption, no stain of suspicion ever fell upon him....This single fact alone is enough to crown him with glory.[3]

Furthermore, in the House of Representatives, close friend and African American Massachusetts State Senator Joshua B. Smith declared in tears that while this nation speaks of Sherman's March to the Sea as incredible, it was nothing compared to Sumner's successes; while Sherman had the nation supporting him, a hundred thousand men, and the wealth of the Union at his feet, Sumner only had "simple justice," fought alone, and had "only the prayers of the poor" in his defeat of slavery.[4]

Not only were elected officials in mourning, but the entire Northern public sphere as well; on March 15, the night before his funeral, there was a public demonstration in the streets that had "never before been witnessed on any similar occasion" as "the tireless stream of humanity passed through the open doors where the great Senator lay in state."[5] All throughout Massachusetts, Charles Sumner was an iconic figure. On Monday, March 16, the day of his funeral, the entire city of Boston shut down. Famous black civil rights leader Frederick Douglass led the funeral procession made up of "vast crowds" and "tens of thousands" from "every part of New England"—all of whom went to pay their respects to Sumner.[6] The Commemorative Volume of Sumner's funeral stated

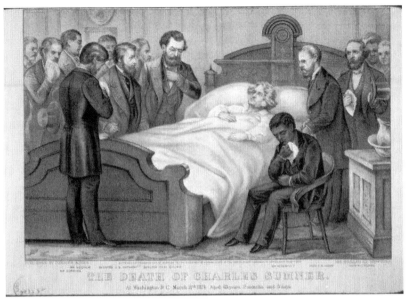

A portrait of Sumner in his death bed, 1874 (Library of Congress)

that every business was suspended, the main streets and shops were closed down and "the city was filled with moving throngs, whose faces expressed the universal sorrow."[7] Following his death, the *New York Times* wrote that, "Sumner displayed a heroism and devotion to principle which has seldom been equaled."[8] Another *New York Times* periodical a week later exclaimed that Sumner's death had been talked about all week and that it was still "too difficult to write upon."[9] Washington, D.C. and the Northern part of the country participated in an unprecedented splendor of mourning.

While Sumner undoubtedly had many faults stemming from his personal character and his political ineptitude, he was an "orator and statesman who ranks with the founding fathers of American democracy."[10] His memory in American history should remain in the upper echelon of civil rights leaders just as it was following his death. Historian Anne-Marie Taylor explained that while no history of the Civil War or Reconstruction would ever leave his name out, the "intellectual outlook and cultural values" that gave him such prominence had been "generally ignored or belittled." Taylor argued that, "America has been robbed of one of her most appealing leaders and inspiring voices."[11] Not only did Sumner have a legacy steeped in social justice during the latter half of the nineteenth century, but his accomplishments also deserve recognition. "To Sumner more than to any single man..." Moorfield Storey wrote in 1900, "the colored race owes its emancipation and such measure of equal rights as it now enjoys."[12] Even more, Sumner's speeches established the initial de-legitimization of "separate but equal" and "foreshadowed the vision of civil rights that we maintain today."[13]

Charles Sumner was not a prototypical politician concerned with his political career (as his opponents claimed he was) nor was he a man who succumbed to the prejudiced restraints of his era. Instead, Sumner was a visionary; he was a man who wholeheartedly believed that until the country offered complete equal rights to blacks in every possible arena, the country would continue to be an inhumane society that slandered the Founders' intent for universal equality. Political shortcomings aside, he should be remembered for his vision, his unique accomplishments, and a life dedicated to civil rights in an unprecedented era.

epilogue

The Reconstruction Era in which Thaddeus Stevens, Ulysses S. Grant, and Charles Sumner lived will forever be one of the most complex, interesting, yet controversial periods in American history. After all, historian Hans L. Trefousse's use of the phrase "America's first effort at interracial democracy" appropriately represents the social experiment that took place following the Civil War.[1] In a matter of years, the country had split into two separate factions (depending on one's interpretation of secession) and then reunited after a bloody war; in result, millions of African Americans who were enslaved were suddenly free. In the years following the Civil War the nation was ushered into an unprecedented era of uncertainty and eventually became an entirely different country than the one it was in 1860—both in terms of social and economic changes.

In terms of civil rights and race relations, Reconstruction set the foundation for America's struggle to secure equal rights for African Americans. The Fourteenth and Fifteenth Amendments as well as the Civil Rights Act of 1875 were extremely important advancements in civil rights. Not only were they symbolic to the freedmen during Reconstruction, but they were responsible for great progressive changes in America; blacks were given "equal protection" under the law—the most basic civil equalities—and shortly thereafter given the right to vote. Today, the Fourteenth Amendment is still heavily invoked and the basis for almost any lawsuit and legislation touching on equal rights in our diverse country. In addition, the Fourteenth Amendment remains one of the most recognizable Amendments in popular culture because of its principles of equality.

The importance of the Fifteenth Amendment specifically granting African Americans the right to vote, is of course, self-explanatory. These statements are all very obvious. However, what seems to have been forgotten is

Civil Rights Act

CIVIL RIGHTS LAW HAS SHARP RACIAL AND POLITICAL IMPACT

Progress and Politics

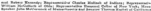

The New Law

A *New York Times* article on July 5, 1964, commemorating the signing of the Civil Rights Act of 1964

that both of these pieces of legislation laid the foundation for future civil rights gains in the 1960s. Yet, rarely is Reconstruction considered the first Civil Rights Movement in public opinion and even rarer does the general public recognize the men who made these monumental pieces of civil rights legislation a reality—Pennsylvania Congressman Thaddeus Stevens and President Ulysses S. Grant.

Even more, the Civil Rights Act of 1875 and the debate surrounding its passage was "nothing less than a crucible in which the thoughts and judgments that would determine the future of race relations were formed."[2] The 1875 Act was the first step to attacking the "separate but equal" clause that would only be defeated over seven decades later in the 1954 *Brown v. Board of Education* Supreme Court decision. In addition, the 1875 Act was the basis for the iconic and famous Civil Rights Act of 1964. For example, a *New York Times* article following the passage of the 1964 Act on July 5, 1964 began by explaining how the 1875 Act gave blacks social equality (though the word social was not used) in public spaces—exactly what the 1964 Act aimed to do.[3] In fact, there are many instances where the 1964 Act has the exact language and wording of its 1875 predecessor. The *New York Times* article stated that President Lyndon Johnson's signing of the bill "was the climax to more than a year of debate, discussion and political maneuvering."[4] While President Johnson and civil rights advocates struggled to fight for such legislation in 1964, imagine what kind of ridicule and struggle Senator Charles Sumner had to go through in 1875—*only twelve years after the end of slavery!*

While the 1960s Civil Rights Movement was initiated by a large-scale movement by blacks who "had defined their rights before bringing their case to government," during Reconstruction, it was "the government that paved the road to political and civil equality" for blacks.[5] And the foremost leaders of government during that time—Stevens, Grant, and Sumner—should be recognized for their courageous and influential role in the "First Civil Rights Movement" just as Dr. Martin Luther King, Jr. and others have appropriately received for what they accomplished in the 1960s. The emotionally hostile and physically dangerous environments in which Stevens, Grant, and Sumner lived far out-weighed the bad environment in the 1960s. As prejudiced as whites had felt about blacks in the years prior to Rosa Parks refusing to change her seat in the middle of the bus, that level of prejudice did not come close to matching the level of bigotry that whites had for blacks who were sold as property and chained like animals only years before Stevens made his impassioned plea for equality. The courage, audacity, and downright dedication that these three men possessed in fighting for essentially the same principles that MLK and other advocates fought for eighty years later is nothing short of extraordinary.

Historian Peter C. Myers argued that the "twentieth century civil rights reforms represent a 'second Reconstruction...'"[6] However, Americans should first recognize the original Reconstruction that changed the course of history in America's Civil Rights struggle. One could argue that if the first civil rights movement did not occur during Reconstruction, then the latter movement of the 1960s would not have progressed so rapidly—or even at all.

This thesis does not attempt to portray Thaddeus Stevens, Ulysses S. Grant, and Charles Sumner as heroes or saints and nor were they; each was a very flawed human being in a variety of different ways as each made decisions that may have hurt the cause they all were trying so hard to protect. They were very far from perfect. Even more, the first civil rights movement that Myers refers to, by many historians' accounts, ultimately failed as a whole. However, that does not discount the great civil rights achievements of these three men. Frankly, the civil rights accomplishments of these three men were real. Their impact on improving the lives of African Americans was important. Their vision and courage in the face of unfathomable circumstances was admirable. And for all of it, they should be remembered.

NOTES

NOTES

NOTES

PREFACE

[1] Joan Waugh, *U.S. Grant*: American Hero, American Myth (Chapel Hill: University of North Carolina Press, 2009), 216.
[2] Fawn M. Brodie, *Thaddeus Stevens: Scourge of the South* (New York: W.W. Norton & Company, Inc., 1959), 9.
[3] Edward Pierce, *The Memoir and Letters of Charles Sumner,* vol. IV (Boston: Roberts Brothers, 1893), 364; George Henry Haines, *Charles Sumner* (Philadelphia: George W. Jacobs & Company Publishers, 1909), 435.
[4] Henry S. Commager and R. B. Morris, *Reconstruction*: America's Unfinished Revolution, ed. Eric Foner (New York: Perennial Classics, 2002), xvi.

CHAPTER ONE: *INTRODUCTION*

[1] Hans Trefousse, *Reconstruction: America's First Effort at Racial Democracy* (New York: Robert E. Krieger Publishing Co., 1964), 12.
[2] Eric Foner, *Reconstruction: America's Unfinished Revolution* (New York: Perennial Classics, 2002), 179.
[3] Ibid, 188-9; Kenneth Stampp, *The Era of Reconstruction: 1865-1877* (New York: Alfred A. Knopf, 1978), 68.
[4] Foner, *Reconstruction,* 197.
[5] Stampp, *Era of,* 82.
[6] Stampp, *Era of,* 118; See Foner, *Reconstruction,* pp. 221-248; See Trefousse, *Reconstruction,* pp. 18-27.
[7] Ibid, 130; See Treffouse, *Reconstruction,* pp. 27; See DuBois pp.

220-230; See Foner, *Reconstruction,* pp. 68-71.

[8] Foner, *Reconstruction,* 233.

[9] Ibid, 267; See also Stampp pp. 135-138; See also Trefousse, *Reconstruction,* pp. 31-34.

[10] Foner, *Reconstruction, 333-334.*

[11] Ibid, 276.

[12] Texas State Library and Archive Commission, *Reconstruction Acts: 1867,*
http://www.tsl.state.tx.us/ref/abouttx/secession/reconstruction.html

[13] Foner, *Reconstruction,* 393-394.

[14] Allan Nevins and Henry S. Commager, *America* (Oxford: Oxford University Press, 1976), 252.

[15] Ibid, 253.

[16] Foner, *Reconstruction,* 423, 425.

[17] Trefousse, *Reconstruction,* 79; For a more in-depth description of the 1876 election, refer to Brooks D. Simpson, *Reconstruction Presidents,* pp. 193-199.

[18] James M. McPherson, *Long-Legged Yankee Lies,* eds. Joan Waugh & Alice Fahs (Chapel Hill: University of North Carolina Press, 2004), 64.

[19] William A. Dunning, *Reconstruction, Political and Economic 1865-1877* (New York: Harper, 1907), 325.

[20] James Ford Rhodes, *History of the United States from the Compromise of 1850,* vol. 7 (New York: 1906), quoted in Kenneth Stamp, *The Era of Reconstruction* (New York: Alfred A. Knopf, 1978), 6.

[21] Ibid, *xvii.*

[22] William A. Dunning, *Essays on the Civil War and Reconstruction* (New York: Harper Torchbooks, 1965), 187, xii.

[23] W.E.B. DuBois, *Black Reconstruction in America* (New York: Antheneum, 1975), 723.

[24] Frances FitzGerald, *America Revised* (New York: Vintage Books, 1980), 85-86.

[25] Kyle Ward, *History in the Making* (New York: The New Press, 2006), xix.

[26] Ibid., 198-9.

[27] Ibid., 201.

[28] Foner, *Reconstruction,* xix.

[29] FitzGerald, *History,* 85.

[30] Ibid.

[31] Ibid, 86.

[32] Foner, *Reconstruction,* xx

[33] Ibid.

[34] Ibid., xxi.

[35] Foner, *Reconstruction,* xxi.

[36] Ibid., xxii.

[37] Joan Waugh, *Personal Communication,* Oct. 14, 2010.

[38] For example, a recent history textbook, *The American People: Creating a Nation and a Society* by John R. Howe, which is already more progressive than many, only mentioned Charles Sumner and Thaddeus Stevens in passing on four and two pages, respectively.

CHAPTER TWO: *THE CREATION OF AN ADVOCATE*

[1] Bruce Chadwick, *The Reel Civil War* (New York: Alfred A. Knopf, 2001), 18; As quoted in *The Reel Civil War*, 132, from *Variety,* February 9, 1949.

[22] Ralph Korngold, *Thaddeus Stevens: A Being Darkly Wise and Rudely Great* (New York: Harcourt, Brace, and Company, 1955), vii.

[3] Foner, *Reconstruction,* 229.

[4] Ibid.

[5] Fawn H. Brodie, *Thaddeus Stevens: Scourge of the South* (New York: W.W. Norton & Company, 1959), 23.

[6] Carter G. Woodson, "Thaddeus Stevens," *Negro History Bulletin,* no. 13 (1949): *51.*

[7] Ibid, 29.

[8] Milton Meltzer, *Stevens and the Fight for Negro Rights (*New York: Thomas Crowell Co., 1967), 73-74.

[9] Korngold, *Thaddeus Stevens,* 9.

[10] Trefousse, *Thaddeus Stevens,* 30.

[11] Brodie, *Thaddeus Stevens,* 33.

[12] Korngold, *Thaddeus Stevens,* 44.

[13] Extensive research has failed to reveal any other type of stain throughout Stevens' life. Korngold explained that Stevens mostly likely felt immense pressure to win his first case before the state supreme court and was probably influenced by the recent passage of the Missouri Compromise to not re-aggravate the issue of slavery.

[14] Brodie, *Thaddeus Stevens,* 33.

[15] *Gettyburg's Sentinel,* July 9, 1823.

[16] Brodie, *Thaddeus Stevens,* 33.

[17] Korngold, 45.

[18] Hans L. Trefousse, *Thaddeus Stevens: Nineteenth-Century Egalitarian* (Chapel Hill: The University of North Carolina Press, 1997), 24; The Anti-Masonic Party was the first "third" political party that focused on opposition to the Freemasons ideology of a secret society.

[19] Ibid, 33.

[20] Trefousse, *Thaddues Stevens,* 33; *Republic Compiler,* "Gettysburg," October 12, 1830: 4.

[21] Treffouse, *Thaddeus Stevens,* 46-47.

[22] *Proceedings and Debates of the Convention of the Commonwealth of Pennsylvania,* vol. 3, (Harrisburg, 1837), 694.

[23] Alexander Hood, "Thaddeus Stevens." *Biographical History of Lancaster County* (Lancaster, PA: Elias Barr, 1872), *579*.
[24] Beverly Wilson Palmer, *The Selected Papers of Thaddeus Stevens* 1 (Pittsburgh: University of Pittsburgh Press, 1997), 85.
[25] Trefousse, *Thaddeus Stevens,* 78.
[26] Thaddeus Stevens, *The Selected Papers of Thaddeus Stevens* 1, ed. Beverly Wilson Palmer (Pittsburgh: University of Pittsburgh Press, 1997), 85.
[27] Stevens, *Papers* I, 132.
[28] Brodie, *Stevens,* 120.
[29] Nicole Etcheson, *Bleeding Kansas: Contested Liberty in the Civil War Era* (Lawrence: University of Kansas, 2004), 23; The Kansas-Nebraska Act of 1854 created the new territories of Nebraska and Kansas, repealed the Missouri Compromise of 1820 and gave each new territory "popular sovereignty" to vote on whether to become a free or slave state.
[30] Brodie, *Stevens,* 126.
[31] Palmer, *Papers,* 87.
[32] Foner, *Reconstruction,* 5.
[33] Brodie, *Stevens,* 115.
[34] Trefousse, *Stevens,* 137, 111.
[35] Stevens, *Papers* I, 253.

CHAPTER THREE: *THE FIGHT FOR THE 14TH AMENDMENT*

[1] Benjamin B. Kendrick, *The Journal of the Joint Committee of Fifteen on Reconstruction* (New York: Columbia University, 1914), 29-30.
[2] Trefousse, *Thaddeus Stevens,* 189.
[3] Eric Foner in *Reconstruction,* pp. 35-27, describes the Ten-Perfect Plan as one of Lincoln's Reconstruction policies; it enabled any Southern state to establish a new state government if at least 10% of its constituency pledged loyalty to the Union.
[4] Meltzer, *Thaddeus Stevens,* 185.
[5] Ibid, 186.
[6] Brodie, *Thaddeus Stevens,* 268.
[7] Thaddeus Stevens, *The Selected Papers of Thaddeus Stevens,* vol. 2, eds. Beverly Wilson Palmer and Holly Byers Ochoa. (Pittsburgh: University of Pittsburgh Press, 1998), 70.
[8] *Congressional Globe,* 39th Congress, 1st Session, 1: 356-358.
[9] Stevens, *Papers* II, 184.
[10] Stevens, *Papers* II, 53.
[11] Ibid, 54.
[12] Kendrick, *Journal of the Joint Committee,* 302.
[13] Brodie, *Thaddeus Stevens,* 268.

[14] Ibid, 271.
[15] Stevens, *The Selected Papers* II, 134.
[16] Stevens, *Selected Papers* II, 135.
[17] Ibid, 269.
[18] *United States National Archives and Records Administration.* Washington, D.C. http://www.archives.gov/exhibits/charters/constitution_amendments_11-27.html
[19] *Congressional Globe,* 39th Congress, 1 session, June 13, 1866, 3148.
[20] Michael J. Perry, *We the People: The Fourteenth Amendment and the Supreme Court (New York: Oxford University Press, 1999),* 55.
[21] Earl M. Maltz, *The Fourteenth Amendment and the Law of the Constitution* (Durham: Carolina Academic Press, 2003), 171.
[22] Ibid, 172.
[23] James E. Bond, *No Easy Walk to Freedom: Reconstruction and the Ratification of the Fourteenth Amendment* (Westport: Praeger, 1997), 272.

CHAPTER FOUR: *OLD THAD STEVENS REMEMBERED*

[1] Foner, *Reconstruction,* 274.
[2] Ibid.
[3] New York Times, 1868.
[4] Nevins and Commager, *America,* 156.
[5] DuBois, *Black Reconstruction,* 342-343.
[6] Stevens, *Selected Papers,* 462.
[7] Meltzer, *Thaddeus Stevens,* 215.
[8] DuBois, *Black Reconstruction,* 344.
[9] *New York Times,* "Thaddeus Stevens," August 13, 1868.
[10] Stevens, *The Papers* II, 469.
[11] Meltzer, *Thaddeus Stevens,* 217.
[12] Trefousse, *Thaddeus Stevens,* 241.
[13] Meltzer, 218.
[14] *New York Times,* "Thaddeus Stevens," August 18, 1868.
[15] Brodie, 366.
[16] Trefousse, *Thaddeus Stevens,* 245.

CHAPTER FIVE: *"THE AMERICAN SPHINX"*

[1] Waugh, 305-306; This entire story is taken from Waugh's book on the memory of U.S. Grant.
[2] Ibid, 2, 303.
[3] John Mosier, *Grant* (New York: Palgrave Macmillan, 2006), 1;

Mosier explained that "There are enough biographies of Ulysses S. Grant to fill a small library" as Grant has been extensively studied in past and in recent analyses.

[4] Ibid, 7.

[5] Brooks D. Simpson, *Ulysses S. Grant: Triumph over Adversity 1822-1865* (New York: Houghton Mifflin Company, 200), xvii.

[6] Bruce Catton, *U.S. Grant and the American Military Tradition* (New York: Gosset and Dunlap, 1954), 179.

[7] Josiah Bunting, *Ulysses S. Grant* (New York: Times Book, 2004), 10.

[8] Ibid, 11.

[9] Simpson, *Grant,* 16.

[10] Ulysses S. Grant, *Personal Memoirs of Ulysses S. Grant* (Lincoln: University of Nebraska Press, 1996), 27.

[11] Waugh, *Grant,* 27; Ulysses S. Grant, *Papers of Ulysses S. Grant,* Vol. 1, ed. John Y. Simon (Carbondale: Southern Illinois University, 1982), xxxviii; The Mexican-American War was a controversial war that President James K. Polk initiated against Mexico to acquire more land. Generally, most pro-slavery people supported the war to expand slavery in the newly acquired land.

[12] Waugh, *U.S. Grant,* 31.

[13] Ibid, 31.

[14] Grant, *Papers* 1, 37.

[15] Jean Edward Smith, *Grant* (New York: Simon & Schuster, 2001), 92.

[16] Grant, *Papers* 1, 339-340.

[17] Waugh, *U.S. Grant,* 42.

[18] Smith, *Grant,* 94.

[19] Grant, *Personal Memoirs,* 129.

[20] Geoffrey Perret, *Ulysses S. Grant* (New York: Random House, 1997), 119.

[21] Waugh, *U.S. Grant,* 52; For a more detailed analysis of Grant's military career—in which there have been almost uncountable volumes—refer to other books such as Geoffrey Perrett, *Ulysses S. Grant*: Soldier and President (New York: Random House, 1997); Robin Neillands, *Grant* (London: Weidenfeld & Nicholson, 2004), or John Mosier's *Grant*.

[22] Perret, 175; Grant, *Robin Neillands* (London: Weidenfeld & Nicholson, 2004), 52-53.

[23] Waugh, *U.S. Grant,* 68.

[24] Ibid, 72.

[25] Grant, *Papers* 8, 342; Waugh, *U.S. Grant,* 73.

[26] Grant, *Papers* 9, 196.

[27] *New York Times,* "SOUTHERN NEWS: Treatment of Captured Negroes Correspondence between Gens. Grant and Lee," November 1, 1864, http://www.nytimes.com

[28] For an in-depth analysis of how Grant planned to conquer Confederate troops, refer to Brooks D. Simpson, *Ulysses S. Grant,* 266-291.

[29] Waugh, *U.S. Grant,* 94-95; Smith, *Grant,* 382; For more details on the final stages of the war in the Eastern Theater, refer to Smith, pp. 370-406.

[30] Simpson, *Ulysses S. Grant,* 436-437.

[31] John Russell Young, *Around the World with General Grant,* vol. 1 (New York: Subscription Book Department, The American News Company, 1879), 416.

[32] Grant, *Papers* 17, 98.

[33] Waugh, *U.S. Grant,* 116.

[34] Grant, *Papers* 18, 292; Bunting, *Ulysses S. Grant,* 81.

CHAPTER SIX: *A VISION FOR SUFFRAGE*

[1] Grant, *Papers* 18, 292; Bunting, *Ulysses S. Grant,* 81.

[2] Grant, *Papers* 19, 87; the Freedmen's Bureau was established by the Department of War in 1865 as a branch of government that was in charge protecting freedmen and provide relief in ways such as a place of refugee shelter, food rationing, and other aid.

[3] Grant, *Papers* 19, 108.

[4] Brooks D. Simpson, *The Reconstruction Presidents* (Lawrence: University Press of Kansas, 1998), 143.

[5] William Gillette, *The Rights to Vote: Politics and Passage of the Fifteenth Amendment* (Baltimore: John Hopkins Pres, 1965), 23.

[6] In the Fourteenth Amendment, the line "race or color" in the second section was removed in reference to who can and cannot vote.

[7] Ibid, 25.

[8] *Congressional Globe,* 39th Congress, 1st Session: 2766.

[9] Gillette, *Right to Vote,* 27.

[10] DuBois, *Black Reconstruction,* 377.

[11] Frank J. Scaturro, *President Grant Reconsidered* (New York: University Press of America, Inc., 1998), 102.

[12] Gillette, *Right to Vote,* 79.

[13] Grant, "First Inaugural Address," *Ulysses S. Grant 1822-1885,* ed. Philip R. Moran (New York: Oceana Publications, Inc., 1968), 21.

[14] Gillette, *Right to Vote,* 80.

[15] George R. Brown, *Reminiscences of Senator William M. Stewart of Nevada* (New York: Neale Publishing Co., 1908), 243.

[16] Simpson, *Reconstruction Presidents,* 142.

[17] Ibid, 143.

[18] Foner, *Reconstruction,* 276.

[19] Ibid, 143; Gillette, *Right to Vote,* 146.

[20] Foner, *Reconstruction,* 143.

[21] Grant, *Ulysses Grant,* 69.

[22] Grant, *Papers* 20, 130-131.

[23] *New York Times,* "The Fifteenth Amendment," April 16, 1870.

[24] *New York Times,* "The Fifteenth Amendment," April 15, 1870.

[25] Waugh, *U.S. Grant,* 139.

CHAPTER SEVEN: *AN UNDESERVING LEGACY*

[1] Simpson, *Reconstruction Presidents,* 153.

[2] Foner, *Reconstruction,* 454-455.

[3] Grant, *Papers* 22, 130.

[4] Ibid, vol. 24, 61.

[5] Ibid, vol. 23, 99; That summer, Grant received a slew of letters from blacks thanking him for all that he had done to secure equal rights thus far as President, 99-100.

[6] Ibid, vol. 23, 290.

[7] For further analysis on these scandals, refer to Jean Edward Smith's *Grant*, pp. 583-585, 590-593, and 552-553.

[8] Foner, *Reconstruction,* 459.

[9] Grant, *Papers* 26, 132.

[10] Ibid, vol. 28, 344.

[11] Grant, *Papers* 28, 62-63.

[12] Simpson, *Reconstruction Presidents,* 196.

[13] Gillette, *Right to Vote,* 9.

[14] To learn about the incredible fight to complete his *Memoirs* in the midst of extreme pain, refer to Waugh's *U.S. Grant,* pp. 167-213.

[15] Waugh, *U.S Grant,* 216.

[16] *Chicago Daily Tribune,* July 24, 1885; James B. Boyd, *Military and Civil Life of Gen.*
Ulysses S. Grant (Philadelphia: P.W. Ziegler & Co., 1885), 677.

[17] *New York Times,* "A Hero Finds Rest," July 24, 1885; Waugh, *U.S Grant,* 216.

[18] *New York Times,* "Eulogies of Gen. Grant," August 10, 1885.

[19] Simpson, *Reconstruction Presidents,* 196.

[20] Scaturro, *Grant Reconsidered,* 12.

[21] Grant, *Papers* 26, 344.

[22] Perret, *Ulysses S. Grant,* 475.

[23] Grant, *Papers* 28, 401.

CHAPTER EIGHT: *A REBEL FROM THE START*

[1] David Donald, *Charles Sumner and The Coming of the Civil War* (New York: Alfred A. Knopf, 1960), vii.

[2] Ibid, vii-viii.

NOTES

Kirt H. Wilson, *The Reconstruction and Desegregation Debate* (East Lansing: Michigan State University Press, 2002), 48.

Beverly Wilson Palmer, *The Selected Letters of Charles Sumner,* ed. Beverly Wilson Palmer (Boston: Northeastern Press, 1990), 3-4.

Donald, *Coming of the Civil War,* 4; In Sumner's own autobiography, he does not write anything about his father, mother, or years growing up in Boston except only to mention that it happened.

Edward Pierce, *The Memoir and Letters of Charles Sumner,* vol. I (Boston: Roberts Brothers, 1893), 58.

Ibid.

Charles Sumner, *The Papers of Charles Sumner* 65, ed. Beverly Wilson Palmer (Alexandra: Chadwyck-Healey, 1988; Microfilm), 023-024.

Anne-Marie Taylor, *Young Charles Sumner* (Amherst: University of Massachusetts Press, 2001), 75.

[10] Ibid, 75; *The Liberator* was a highly controversial abolitionist newspaper that was read by mostly blacks that circulated until 1865.

[11] Charles Sumner, *The Selected Letters of Charles Sumner,* ed. Beverly Wilson Palmer (Boston: Northeastern Press, 1990), 290.

[12] Wilson, *Desegregation,* 48.

[13] Moorfield Storey, *Charles Sumner* (Boston and New York: Houghton Mifflin Company, 1900), 35.

[14] Charles Sumner, "The True Grandeur Of Nations," *Orations and Speeches* (Boston: Ticknor, Reed, and Fields, 1850), 122-123.

[15] Wilson, *Desegregation,* 49.

[16] Nevins and Commager, *America,* 190.

[17] Eric Foner, *Free Soil, Free Labor, Free Men* (New York: Oxford University Press, 1970), 124-125; The Free Soil Party was a third political party from 1848 -1852 whose platform focused on the opposition of extending slavery in the U.S. at all costs.

[18] Charles Sumner, *Argument of Charles Sumner, Esq., Before the Supreme Court of Massachusetts In The Case of Sarah C. Roberts vs. The City of Boston* (Washington: F. & J. Rives & Geo. A. Bailey, 1870), 11, http://ia360612.us.archive.org/3/items/equalitybeforela00sumn/equalitybeforela00sumn.pdf

[19] Leonard W. Levy and Harlan B. Philips, "The Roberts Case: Source of the "Separate by Equal" Doctrine," *The American Historical Review* 56, no. 3 (1951): 512-513, http://www.jstor.org.

[20] Passed as part of the Compromise of 1850, the Fugitive Slave Act declared that all runaway slaves be returned to their masters in the South; Donald, *The Coming of the Civil War,* 232.

[21] Sumner, *Works,* vol. 2, 93.

[22] Charles Sumner, *The Crime against Kansas. The apologies for the crime. The true remedy. Speech of Hon. Charles Sumner, 19th and 20th May , 1856* (Boston: John P. Jewett & Company, 1856), 5.

121

[23] *New York Times,* "Latest Intelligence," May 2, 1856, http://query.nytimes.com; Storey, *Charles Sumner,* 147-148.

[24] Ibid, 299.

[25] Pierce, *Memoir,* 43.

[26] Donald, *The Coming of the Civil War,* 388.

[27] Eric Foner, *Reconstruction* (New York: Perennial Classics, 2002), 61.

[28] David Donald, *Charles Sumner and the Rights of Man* (New York: Alfred A. Knopf, 1970), 49.

[29] Ibid, 49-50.

[30] Ibid, 96.

[31] Sumner, *Selected Letters of Charles Sumner,* 247.

CHAPTER NINE: *THE "CROWNING WORK" OF RECONSTRUCTION*

[1] Donald, *Rights of Man,* 248.

[2] Ibid, 263; For a more in-depth analysis of Sumner's fight against the Fourteenth Amendment and the problems he caused in the Senate, refer to pp. 244-267.

[3] Ronald B. Jager, "Charles Sumner, the Constitution, and the Civil Rights Act of 1875," *The New England Quarterly Inc.* 42, no. 3 (1969): 362, http://www.jstor.org/stable/363614.

[4] *Congressional Globe,* 42 Congress, 2nd Session, December 2, 1871: 244.

[5] Foner, *Reconstruction,* 504.

[6] Donald, *Rights of Man,* 531.

[7] Foner, *Reconstruction,* 504.

[8] Donald, *the Rights of Man,* 537;

[9] *Congressional Globe,* 42nd Congress, 2nd Session, 1872: 381.

[10] Ibid, 382.

[11] Ibid.

[12] Pierce, *Memoir,* 504.

[13] Charles Sumner, *The Works of Charles Sumner.* Vol. XV. Executed by Francis V. Balch (Boston: Lee and Shephard, 1883), 267. Sumner is referring to the Washington Monument, which at the time, was only partially completed due to the Civil War and subsequent construction hiatus'.

[14] Ibid, 268-269.

[15] Ibid, 305.

[16] Du Bois, *Black Reconstruction in America,* 594; Donald, *Rights of Man,* 587.

[17] Wilson, *Desegregation,* 33.

[18] Bertram Wyatt-Brown, "The Civil Rights Act of 1875," *Political Research Quarterly* 18 (1965): 769. However, other historians such as

Michael McConnell argued that Sumner's death had little to do with the bill's passage.

[19] Foner, *Reconstruction,* 532.

[20] Wilson, *Desegregation,* 35.

[21] *Civil Rights Act of 1875, U.S. Statutes at Large* 18 (1875): 335-337.

[22] Wilson, *Desegregation,* 45.

[23] Foner, *Reconstruction*, 556; For more information on the enforcement of the 1875 Act, refer to John Hope Franklin, "The Enforcemnt of the Civil Rights Act of 1875," *Prologue,* 6 (Winter 1974), 227.

[24] Ibid.

[25] Ibid, 15.

CHAPTER TEN: *A CIVIL RIGHTS LEADER AHEAD OF HIS TIME*

[1] Storey, *Charles Sumner,* 86.

[2] A *Memorial of Charles Sumner* (Boston: Commonwealth of Massachusetts, 1874), 7; This volume contains thirty-seven pages worth of orations from Senators and Congressmen on the "greatness" of the late Charles Sumner.

[3] Ibid, 18-19.

[4] Ibid, 60; "Sherman's March to the Sea" was an offensive attack against the Confederacy by Union General William Tecumseh Sherman in which he captured both Atlanta and the Savannah port.

[5] Ibid, 72.

[6] DuBois, *Black Reconstruction,* 594.

[7] Ibid, 73.

[8] *The New York Times,* "Charles Sumner," March 12, 1874.

[9] *The New York Times,* "Charles Sumner: Some Reminiscences of the Deceased Statesman," March 17, 1874.

[10] Louis Ruchames, "The Pulitzer Prize Treatment of Charles Sumner," *The Massachusetts Review* 2, no. 4 (1961): 769.

[11] Taylor, *Young Charles Sumner,* 1.

[12] Storey, *Charles Sumner,* 432.

[13] Wilson, *Desegregation,* 56.

EPILOGUE

[1] Hans L. Trefousse titles his book on Reconstruction *Americas First Effort at Racial Democracy.*

[2] Wilson, *Desegregation,* 15.

[3] *New York Times,* "Civil Rights Act," July 5, 1964.

[4] Ibid.

[5] Scaturro, *Grant Reconsidered,* 93.

[6] Peter C. Myers, *Frederick Douglass: Race and the Rebirth in American Liberalism* (Lawrence: University Press of Kansas, 2008), 4.

INDEX

INDEX

125

INDEX

127

ABOUT THE AUTHOR

Barry M. Goldenberg is a recent graduate of UCLA, magna cum laude, with a Bachelor of Arts in History and a Minor in Education Studies. He is currently pursuing a Master of Arts in Sociology and Education in the Department of Education Policy and Social Analysis at Teachers College, Columbia University in the City of New York.

To learn more, visit http://www.barrygoldenberg.com.

ABOUT CRITICAL MINDS PRESS

Critical Minds Press is a publishing company for emerging scholars interested in issues related to social justice and a network of people committed to the future. Including authors from all disciplines, Critical Minds Press seeks to give previously unpublished authors the opportunity to share their works, thoughts, and essays with the world—in hopes of making it a better place.

CRITICAL MINDS PRESS

Made in the USA
Lexington, KY
08 January 2013